LEGAL DISCLAIMER

ADRIAN'S DISCLAIMER

Let's Make a Deal: In return for the knowledge contained within these pages, you agree that I am in no way recommending or offering to sell you any of the investments listed in this book. For that matter, I have not received any compensation from any of the organizations mentioned in this book.

You are very, very smart. And as a very smart person, you are responsible for how you spend and invest your money.

Deal?
Deal.

Disclosure: At time of writing I am invested in or with:

American Homeowner Preservation (AHP)
Pattern Energy (PEGI)
Brookfield Renewable Partners (BEP)
Aspiration Redwood and Flagship Funds (REDWX, ASPFX)
Amalgamated Bank
CNote
SONDORS Electric Car

By the way, I'm not recommending or offering any of these investments.

The Do-Gooder's Guide to Investing

Adrian Reif is a social entrepreneur and investor dedicated to building a better world.

He began his career in finance where he witnessed the power of the capital markets to help our planet sink—or swim. While vagabonding through Asia, Adrian sank his teeth into an epiphany on his trek to Everest Base Camp. He returned home with $80 left in his bank account to launch Yumbutter, an organic nut butter company on a mission. After several years of missteps, the company grew to become the leading socially-conscious nut butter company in the country, and has provided over 1 million nutritional feedings to children with malnutrition through its BuyOne:FeedOne™ business model. His 2015 TEDx Talk shared his belief that through your everyday actions you can change the course of history.

Adrian is a thinker creating new models to solve existential problems. His current work focuses on expanding human potential so we can love more and create massive impact. He has gone on to launch Incredible Design Studio, a company making beautiful products from ocean plastic, and Tree Latte, the premier tree planting membership in the world, with a mission to plant 1 billion trees in the next 10 years.

He lives in a small mountain town in Colorado with his wife where he takes ice baths thanks to Wim Hof, skis, bikes, and paddleboards on whitewater.

This book is an invitation to one million people to shift *just* $10,000 to investments that are better for people and the planet. Collectively, that's $10 billion for a better world. Adrian will be your friend if you join in.

AdrianReif.com
Follow @ Facebook.com/Adrian.Reif
Instagram: @adrian_on_spaceshipearth

100% of profits invested in:

- Transformative companies with embedded social and environmental impact
- Regenerative farming & land conservation
- Affordable housing development

The
Do-Gooder's Guide
to
Investing

Grow Your Money While
Investing in Communities, Renewables,
Affordable Housing, and More

Adrian Reif

**Founder of Yumbutter &
Incredible Design Studio**

First printing, 2019

Cover design by Alison Davis
Book design & layout by Polgarus Studio

Cedar & Sage Press
Colorado, USA

Dedicated to the do-gooding entrepreneurs, activists, and rabble rousers making the world a bit happier and healthier, especially those of you featured in this book.

Contents

Dear reader,

For the past decade, I've watched the world change.

Watched it wake up. It's a beautiful thing.

I've changed, too. A little braver, if nothing else. Brave enough to write this book, at least. Brave enough to share my hopes of a better world for everyone.

At the same time, I continue to see frustration among friends and peers. Change isn't happening fast enough.

At the end of the day, our hearts ask, "Did I make a difference?" Sometimes we can answer "yes." Others times we feel a defeated "no."

The truth is, regardless of how you answer, you *can* make a difference. You *do* make a difference, every day. Each thought, every action ripples out shaping the future of humanity and this wondrous planet. In fact, as you'll find out in the pages ahead, you play an undeniable role in shaping the future.

This book was born from asking, "What if the average person could do more? Make a bigger difference with something as simple as where they keep their money?"

As an entrepreneur and investor for the last decade, I've been fortunate to see a world teeming with do-gooders doing amazing things. Building solar farms, conserving land, resurrecting fisheries, educating folks around the world. What if your bank account could accelerate these efforts? What if we could simplify the powerful and practical act of investing with purpose?

So here it is. A lifetime of experience, three years of research, and one seed of hope: that we can build the world we want to live in.

I'm honored to share my humble lessons and grateful to be on the journey with you.

Big love,
Adrian

Colorado, USA

SOME HOUSEKEEPING NOTES THAT MIGHT HELP

Fantastic Beasts and Where to Find Them

The investing world is filled with fantastically strange beasts. Some pull CO2 right out of the air and practically turn it into money. Quite magical, if you ask me. This is a book about how to find them.

But first, there are some things you should know before we enter this world together.

1. For Beginners to Advanced

Unlike other investing books, this book is for *everyone*. Whether you know all about investing, or you're just getting started, there's something here for you. Investing lingo is kept to a minimum so the information in this book can be accessible to all. For investing newbies, there's an Investing Primer at the beginning of Part 3. For experienced investors, the book offers new perspectives on sustainable investing from both a moral and fiduciary lens. Experienced investors—some managing multi-million dollar portfolios—have gained new insights and learned about investments and strategies—like Ray Dalio's All-Weather portfolio strategy in Part 3—that have become extremely valuable.

2. Comprehensive

Dense, some might say. Whatever.

I'll admit, early readers were surprised to find over 100 investing options waiting for them in Part 2. Instead of paring it back, I decided to keep them because I want this book to be the go-to reference for sustainable investments—a handy guide that can be opened for inspiration or ideas.

However, the book is organized such that if you're intrigued by Affordable Housing, you can flip to that chapter and soak up all the knowledge. Personally, I find every investment in this book interesting because each one symbolizes an opportunity where money can flow to solve a massive problem. And we need more of these solutions.

A note on the sustainable investment universe: Do I cover every sustainable investment on the market? I tried. This book includes about 90% of the sustainable investing options out there. I left out investments that are either a) debatably impactful, like peer-to-peer lending or b) too challenging to access that most readers would not be able to use them.

Keep in mind the investing universe can change quickly. Several new investments popped up over the three years writing this book. That's why I built a living database at www.adrianreif.com/dogoodersguide .

Another reason—a selfish one, perhaps—I include so many investing options is I'm continually in awe at the amazing initiatives, companies, and efforts of our fellow humans. I invite you to be curious and be amazed with me—organic farmland investors, a company keeping people in their homes, and people revitalizing poor communities with art. Who wouldn't geek out to that!?

3. Choose Your Own Adventure

I secretly wish I could have put this on the cover.

"YOU'RE THE STAR OF THE STORY!
CHOOSE FROM 40 POSSIBLE ENDINGS"[1]

But investing has infinite possible endings. The design of your portfolio should suit you, no one else. This book is designed so you can skip around as needed.

Here's a snapshot of the book so you can chart your course.

Part 1 | Part 1 unpacks sustainable investing and demystifies the main questions.

Part 2 | Part 2 is organized by themes like affordable housing, stock market, and renewable energy. Each chapter provides a snapshot of individual investments, with a review at the end of each chapter.

Part 3 | Part 3 guides you through creating your own personalized do-

---

[1] Lifted from the cover of an old choose your own adventure children's book.

gooder portfolio, with real-world examples from fellow do-gooders and professional, world-class investors. It also distinguishes between the four investing destinations—getting rich quick, short-term investing, long-term investing, and preservation of existing money—and offers suggestions for making them a little more, or a lot more, sustainable.

4. Accredited vs. Non-accredited Investors

Jargon alert But this is an important one to know. Plus, you'll sound extra fancy at the next cocktail party as you espouse on the philosophical merits of opening the private capital markets to non-accredited investors.

In short, "accredited" investor is a term created by our investing regulatory bodies that defines someone having over $1 million in assets (minus the worth of their primary home) *or* have earned more than $200,000 per year for the last two years (or $300,000 combined with spouse). These folks get access to investment deals that are private and unregistered with financial authorities. The intention of these rules assumed these individuals could risk the cash, while us poor folks could not.

"Non-accredited" investors—what I call *everyday* investors—earn less than $200,000 in a year or have less than $1 million in assets. Thanks to the passage of crowdfunding regulations, these folks can now access deals once reserved for 1-percenters.[2]

Since the purpose of this book is to empower the everyday investor, the majority of investments in this book are available to non-accredited investors. I do list several accredited-only investments and have marked them as such.

5. Let's Have Some Fun

Investing is a serious topic—we're talking real money here. But I've slogged through too many investing books with heavy eyelids. Perhaps this is why so many people are scared to death of investing. But investing *is* mind-blowingly interesting, especially when you add positive impact to the mix.

What you have is a book filled with the latest research, data, and interest

---

[2] There are still limits on the amount of money they can invest in one year, so Joe-Smoe doesn't pump his median-wage paycheck into what he thinks is going to be the next Facebook. See *Angel Investing and Crowdfunding* chapter for more.

rates—out of respect for the seriousness of investing. But you also get light notes and attempts at humor,[3] with the intention to make investing a bit more accessible and applicable to daily life.

If you're a serious person, please forgive me. If you choose to put it down, don't worry. It's me, not you.

---

[3] Hey, did you see the word *comedian* in my bio? Cut me some slack.

" THE STONE AGE DIDN' T
END FOR LACK OF
STONE. IT ENDED
BECAUSE PEOPLE' S
IMAGINATIONS
CHANGED."

— DJ SPOOKY

PART 1

**WHERE WE'VE BEEN, WHERE WE ARE,
AND WHERE WE CAN GO**

INTRODUCTION

In 2011, I took my first steps on the island of Haiti. Even before landing, I was in awe. As I peered out the airplane window, the flight over one island revealed two worlds. To the east, the Dominican Republic, denoted by a lush, green landscape that reached to the middle of the island. Then, an unmistakable line where the greenery stops, and a deforested, moon-like landscape begins. I asked a fellow passenger over the din of the prop engines, "What's that?"

"The border," they responded. But the demarcation marks more than a border. It marks a history of subjugation and imbalance and supposed leaders who've failed their people.

I came to Haiti to visit a potential non-profit partner for my company, Yumbutter, that could help us with the BuyOne:FeedOne arm of our business. For every Yumbutter product sold, we'd help feed a child with malnutrition. Our goal was to maximize positive impact, so starting in the most malnourished country in our hemisphere made the most sense.[4]

At that point, landing in Haiti would be the 13th country I'd been to—not a worldly soul, but not a sheltered one either.

Malnutrition was visible, everywhere. Rubbled buildings from the earthquake a year earlier were out of a movie. Trash filled canals, often smoking as fire or flood were the only options for removal. Motorbikes bounced over unpaved roads, often unpaved because aid money had been siphoned away by bureaucrats.

One afternoon, on a walk down the dusty road back to my apartment, in a small lane between crumbling brick buildings, I stopped to watch three young boys play basketball. They tossed the dust-coated ball upward toward a bottomless crate tacked to a pole. Amid what *I* called devastation, these little souls laughed and played and ribbed each other like any other children in the world. Their smiles, curved ear to ear, as big as any I'd ever seen.

---

[4] Over 9 years later, it has helped provide over 1 million feedings & medical intervention for children in need in Haiti and Guatemala.

These smiles are my fondest memory. Even on my darkest days, I remember these smiles. Here, among the brutality, I witnessed the paragon of humanity—inalienable joy.

That day, I took a vow. I'd never—*ever*—stop believing in each person's immutable goodness.

Smiles Make the World Go 'Round

This book exists because of those smiles. And the smiles of hundreds of strangers I've met while wandering this wondrously weird planet. Like a smile, this book is a simple expression of our human desire to always *do a little better*.

People are good. People are great, actually. And yet, somehow, our world is in a bad way. I don't see this as a problem with us—I see it as a problem of *cultural imagination*. We are products of our cultures. Culture tells you what to believe and what's possible and how the world works. For the last 200 years or so, the world has changed *rapidly*. Like horses-to-supersonic-jets-in-50-years rapidly. For those years, a cultural imagination rooted in industriousness and independence served us well.

Times have changed. The world—and perhaps our own consciousness—isn't able to healthily carry everything the last 200 years have brought.

A Search For Answers

For the past decade, I've been on a search for answers. Asking, "How can we create a new imagination?" It started after I quit my job with one of the world's largest banks and spent a year following Rolf Potts' advice and vagabonded myself across Asia, with his book *Vagabonding* tucked in my bag. China, Mongolia, Tibet, Nepal, Thailand, Laos. I told myself I'd keep traveling until I stopped having fun or I ran out of money.

A year later, I landed back in the States with $80 in my bank account. I took it and the cash from a few side gigs and bought peanuts, a food processor, and a mini-course on Photoshop. By the end of my first summer I'd sold $30,000 worth of fresh, organic, handmade peanut butter by setting up shop at five farmers' markets every week.

Five years later, Yumbutter was carried in something like 3,000 grocery stores like the Willy St. Co-op, Whole Foods and Target. The company was a new breed of business, one that endeavored to create the world I want to live in. 300% carbon neutral. Certified B Corp. And creator of BuyOne:FeedOne™, a new model for helping the most impoverished.

While I'd love to end with *happily ever after*, the business was burning cash and I was burning out. I stepped out of my role as CEO while my business partner continued growing the business. Ultimately, the ultra-competitive food industry finally forced us to sell our young company. Luckily, we found someone who'd carry on the mission, while bringing more money to the table. But I felt like I'd failed, both growing the business and creating massive impact.

In the years that followed, I began to realize that my decade of entrepreneurship put me face-to-face with investors, innovators, and large amounts of money. I began to wonder, "What if we could make it easy to shift massive amounts of money to really good things?"

I wanted to shift our cultural imagination to show that we can indeed build a world were people and planet thrive. This massive shift would need massive amounts of money. In short, I would need a massive lever.

The First Class Lever

This is a First Class Lever.

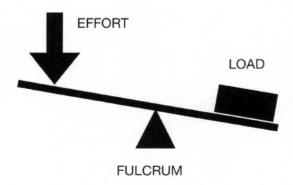

We know that a lever can be used to lift heavy things, or launch a sibling from a seesaw. What if we replaced "effort" with "money" and load with "planetary challenges"? "Fulcrum" becomes "values." Now there's a good looking lever.

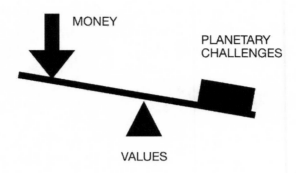

Show Me the Money

"But Adrian, money is evil," they will say.

I'm a stickler for accuracy, and that phrase reeks of overindulgence. Money is not inherently evil. Money is no more or less evil than the water that causes a landslide to come crashing down on houses.

Money is a tool. A force signifying an effort. A hammer swung properly can build a house. A hammer swung violently can tear it down. For the most part, money is simply lazy. It follows the path of least resistance, usually by the hand of she who wields it.

As people around the world wake up, they want to use their money for good. Fortunately, there are more people doing good in the world than ever. Feeding others, building schools, curing cancer. Some companies are becoming better actors. Indeed, these acts are reshaping the course of history.

With this is mind, I set my sights on money. **If money is a tool, it can move the biggest lever the world has seen.** It can solve massive challenges when the world needs it most.

The beauty of investing is that you can invest your money and the money grows, a win-win for you and the organizations you invest in.

Do-Gooder Investing

This brings us to you. And this book. If you picked up this book, chances are you want to do some good. Knowing you, you already have and you're back for more. You've had a sneaking suspicion your money plays an important role, too, and you're wondering if it's possible to align your money and your ideals.

There are millions of people like you. (No, no, of course *you* are special and *you* are the only one like you.[5]) What I mean is that there are millions—heck, maybe even billions—of people around the world who truly want to make the world a better place. But how?

I've been investing, studying markets, and following economies for almost 20 years. Over the last 10 years, I've answered this question for myself and this book will answer it for you:

How can I align my money and my ideals?

I call this *do-gooder investing*. (It's also called other things, like sustainable investing, which I'll explain ahead.) Do-gooder investing is a burgeoning movement that allows *everyday people* to grow their money while investing with purpose. Until recently, it's been veiled behind myths and rumors, obscured by financial lingo, and innocently overlooked by even the saints among us. The biggest movers have been large asset managers—foundations or endowments that invest big chunks of money—like the Bill and Melinda Gates Foundation. Now, I want to bring the secrets of do-gooder investing to everyday investors like you and me.

Even the most willing came to it slowly, but the movement is picking up steam. Decades ago, Desmond Tutu along with others against apartheid in South Africa called for divestments from companies doing business in South Africa, which played a role in the dismantling of apartheid in the country. Many years later, in 2012, Unity College was one of first institutions to sell their shares in coal, oil, and gas companies. From here, the pace picked up. In 2018, the 1000th divestment announcement came from French and Australian pension funds.

Today, responsible investing is booming, and the options are, dare I say, abundant. But more options add complexity. In the pages ahead you'll find straight talk that demystifies do-gooder investing. I'll show you 100+ ways to make money while investing with purpose, show you real-world portfolios from fellow do-gooders, and even show you how to craft your

_____

[5] Dodged a bullet there, eh?

own custom portfolio with help from the best investors in the world. Yes, your very own First Class lever that will move the world.

If we get this right, the world will look a lot cleaner, happier, and safer for ourselves and our children in the years to come.

What is Do-Gooder Investing?

"Sustainable" means maintaining a *certain level*. If the Earth craps out because we sucked it dry, that's obviously not sustainable.

So, what does that look like for us and our planet? A lot of smart people around the globe put their heads together and collectively defined "sustainability" as a path to meet the needs of the present without compromising future generations' ability to meet their own.

> **Global Definition of Sustainability**: A path to meet the needs of the present without compromising future generations' ability to meet their own.[6]

Sustainability, Upgraded

But is sustainability enough? Some of my friends don't believe we can simply *maintain*. To them, the word sustainable suggests keeping things the way they are, or "status quo." Think about it: Who wants a marriage that's just "sustainable"?

At the edges of these growing movements are people who **eschew the idea of "sustainability" for new models deemed "regenerative" or "restorative"[7]** that emphasize the need to *renew* or *restore* our planet, not just sustain it. Since the planet is a bit out of whack, simply sustaining it may not do.

While I agree with this notion, I think we can use a more expansive definition of "sustainable" and forego the rhetorical seesaw. At the end of the day, I think we'd all agree we need to live in balance with a healthy planet, filled with healthy people. So, when we talk about do-gooding and sustainability, here's what we mean.

The Do-Gooder's Definition of Sustainability is something that:

---

[6] UN World Commission on Environment and Development

[7] If you want to learn more, search "regenerative" or "restorative" economics, design, and agriculture. Many of the organizations in this book actually harness restorative models.

1. Stops continued ecological destruction.
2. Regenerates & restores the Earth and natural ecosystems.
3. Creates a safer, happier, healthier life for our fellow humans.

Investing, Upgraded

It turns out sustainability takes effort. As the demands for sustainable methods of generating power, making stuff, and increasing well-being grow, these efforts need capital. Big wads of sustainable moola.

Investing offers a beautiful model that can direct this moola to sustainable efforts while generating something in return for the givers of that capital.

By definition, "investing" is giving your money to some venture in *expectation* of a future return. A good investment will grow your money over time.

Apply this to sustainability, and it turns out that **you can give your money to a project positively impacting the world with the goal of earning a financial return.**

If you're like me and you want to grow your money while moving the world towards a happier, healthier future, sustainable investing is like mocha icing on a coconut milk ice cream cake.

A Rose by Any Other Name

Sustainable investing and *do-gooder investing* are often called other names, but they still smell as sweet.

Socially Responsible Investing.
Impact Investing.
ESG Investing.
Purpose-Driven Investing.
Mission-Driven Investing.
Natural Investing.
Community Investing.
Giving a Damn.[8]

To people in the field, the different terms can have slightly different definitions. For this book's purposes, I use these terms interchangeably.

---

[8] Let's just call it what it is.

Values Investing

Long before Senator Cory Booker jumped in the presidential race for 2020, the first African-American Senator from New Jersey and former Newark Mayor was asked how should an engaged citizen who is becoming overwhelmed and cynical should respond in today's age. He said, "It's so helpful if you can get up everyday and *know* 'What's my purpose today? Who am I? What are my values?'"

Advice taken, Cory.

I've witnessed people all around world begin to live closer to their values. Investing should be no different.

One face of this movement is Margot Seigle, a 28-year-old community organizer who works on a farm in Falls Village, Connecticut. A few years ago, her family's lumber company was sold. Margot asked for advice from both her family's financial advisor as well as her friends as she decided how to invest the money.

"I'm in the process of shifting my investments not just into socially responsible investments but into investments that are investing in the new economy," she said.

Margot was looking at one investment in particular that aligned with her values. The Black Mesa Water Coalition is led by young people in Arizona and helps organize Navajo and Hopi communities to protect their lands and waters. As a response to coal mining that damaged land and water, Black Mesa was looking to develop a solar project on an abandoned coal mine.

Margot's family's financial advisors suggested staying away from "risky" investments like this. However, Margot didn't agree.

"Their bottom line is to make me money," she said. "What's important to me is I'm investing my money in communities and in people."[i]

Margot's philosophy is ever more popular, especially among younger generations. This has caused a big upheaval in the financial world as 66% of children fire their parents' financial advisor after an inheritance. Perhaps this is well deserved. Margot's generation is inheriting a lot of local and global challenges, and they are not afraid to think differently to solve them.

A Values Declaration

What's my purpose today? Who am I? What are my values?

When Sen. Booker asked these questions above, did you have an answer?

If not, I invite you to take a few moments and answer these questions. Not only will it provide clarity in what you stand for and help rise above the fray every morning, it will also be a guiding star as you learn about sustainable investing options, and potentially help guide your investment decisions.

When I asked a handful of do-gooders these questions they answered:

"My purpose is to care for my family and friends."

"I care about staying engaged and growing throughout life."

"I would like to help solve climate change and air pollution."

"I care most about physical, emotional, and spiritual health."

"My purpose is making the world more safe, loving, beautiful and sustainable for my children, your children, and all the children to come."

I found each of these declarations particularly beautiful not solely because of their compassion and care, but also because of the clarity of purpose they give each person.

Since I began the journey of applying investing to sustainability over a decade ago, a lot has changed. Yet, our capacity to care and our need to heal the planet is greater than ever. Let's see what sustainable investing can do for you and the planet.

Answering Your Concerns

Before I typed the first word for this book, I wanted to find out how people like you felt about sustainable investing. I surveyed hundreds of people about their investing experience and asked if sustainability played a factor. Then, I dove in deep with dozens of conversations to learn more.

I chatted with a young professional, a change-the-world glimmer in her eye. I spoke to a calloused retiree who had "seen it all." Another individual manages a $15 million portfolio with a strong emphasis on positive *impact* and taught me a few things.

What did I learn from this wide-ranging crew? And how could I use it to help millions of other do-gooders rethink their own investing?

In the end, two common threads emerged, despite the wildly diverse group of do-gooders. The first thread centered on a question I've witnessed across humanity: *How can I matter?* Each person, in their own way, wants to make a difference. However, as I probed deeper into where sustainable investing falls into the mix, I was surprised. Despite an explicitly clear intention to use their money for good, every person was hamstrung from investing sustainably by just a few concerns. So I focused my research on finding the answers to their questions.

Thread 1: How Can I Matter?

Every single person I interviewed asked some form of the same question: *How can I matter?*

Just as we glance to the same stars each night, every one of us is born with an inalienable right. Life, liberty, and the pursuit of happiness, yes, but let's take it one step further. These rights are hollow if not for the *meaning* we use to fill them up. I'm talking purpose. And purpose comes from taking action in line with our beliefs.

So, how *do* you matter?

Well, more than you can know, in fact. **Our thoughts and actions are the grist of the world.** You impact your friends, your family, the world around you, and those who will come after you.

Despite our celestial desire to matter and the undeniable fact that we shape the world, there are times when we behave like we *don't* matter. When the world seems like it's on fire and our drop of water won't help. I can relate. It's easy to feel lost, helpless. Unable to be the change.

So, before we go any further, let's take some freakin' pressure off of ourselves: *You* don't have to change the world. That's right, no need to outpace Mother Teresa on building schools in Calcutta. No need to hire a barge and scuba gear and spend your vacay pulling plastic out of the Great Pacific Garbage Patch.[9] We each have a role to play. And for many of us it might be as simple as flashing a big smile when you walk into the office, dropping a home-cooked meal with a neighbor in need, or guiding mentees through challenges.

As this thread of meaning unwound itself from the conversations I had, I felt delighted. It speaks to a collective awakening. Perhaps none of these folks will cure cancer, yet they'll impact the world nonetheless.

Of course, we also need those of you who are called to stand on the steps of a capitol building until justice is served. Or go undercover to bust up child slavery rings. Or cure cancer.[10]

In the pages ahead, I hope to offer another small act that can help you live with meaning and purpose. But first, let's explore just why sustainable investing has been at so many fingertips, yet left undone.

Thread 2: "I'm Unsure"

Trust me, I'd have been even more delighted if the common threads had stopped with a desire to matter. My case would be closed, problem solved, world crisis averted. But that wasn't the whole story. These are humans we're talking about after all. So, while we all desire to make a difference in the world, one thing also holds us back: we're unsure.

We're unsure where to start. Or how to do it. Or even what the right thing is in the first place. I know this feeling all too well.

Heck, investing is confusing enough. Now we're supposed to know which companies we invest in emit toxic sludge, hire child labor, or clear-cut Amazonian rainforests?!

---

[9] Hey, don't get me wrong, we'd love you if you did. But a stress-free, happier you is way more effective than a defeated one.
[10] Go you. We've got your back!

We care, but there's a tall chain-link fence posted with a "Keep Out" sign between us and taking action. Three very clear uncertainties emerged regarding sustainable investing, and like most things tucked in the closet, it'll be better if we just talk about them.

Concern 1: Is it profitable?

Many do-gooders are afraid sustainable investing is not financially competitive to less-sustainable investing. They don't want to put their money—and potential financial future—at risk.

Concern 2: Does it actually create a positive impact?

Do-gooders are unsure of the difference they could actually make with sustainable investing.

Concern 3: Utter confusion

Sustainable investing options are hard to find, or confusing, leaving do-gooders overwhelmed and unable to take action.

Truth Seeking

I understand these concerns. They were the same ones that drove my curiosity a decade ago. In that time, I sought the truth, even if I didn't like it. Is every investment in this book wildly profitable? No. Does every seemingly do-gooder investment create tangible change? No.

Yet, emerging evidence, added attention, and brand-new investments point to a promising reality for your money and our planet.

Concern #1: Is it Profitable?

You want to grow your hard-earned money. There's no shame in that. I do, too. Money is an important tool, not only for survival, but for living the life you want to live. You deserve to enjoy life, take care of your loved ones, retire stress-free. Why should you take a risk on investments that you're unsure about? If this is one of your concerns, you may be in for a surprise.

Sustainable investing can provide similar returns to traditional investing, often reducing risk—the inevitable ups and downs—along the way.

OK, but how do we make sure things measure up? What is the methodology used to ensure that sustainable investments are as profitable as less-sustainable investments?

Apples to Apples

Comparing investments isn't easy. Each one has different *risk* and *return*. So, I've tried to compare apples to apples by comparing long-term investments with other long-term investmnets; short-term with short-term; and low-risk with low-risk. Some of the comparisons are very straightforward. For example, American Homeowner Preservation, a fixed-return investment featured in the Affordable Housing chapter, generates a 10% return every year for five years, with minimal risk. Other investments, like the Reinvestment Fund, generate returns up to 4.5% and have a 100% payback history. When we start building portfolios in Part 3, you can see how these stack up simply by comparing them with similar investments.

When it comes to the stock market, many of you will have investments in 401Ks and other stock market investments. Thankfully, there is rich, quantifiable data, with more coming out every year as more attention is given to sustainable investing. When can use this to try and compare funds with similar goals, like these two long-term investments.

The table below compares the returns of two sustainable index funds with "the market"—the S&P 500—over a recent 10-year period. The S&P 500 is the standard measure of "the market" since it contains 500 of the largest companies in the U.S. It's also the recommended investing strategy for passive investors like Warren Buffet, who advise others to "buy and hold the market." In the example below, the Vanguard FTSE Social Index (VFTNX), which is considered by analysts as one of the best socially conscious funds, performed better than the S&P 500 in five out of the ten years. The fund (see A More Sustainable Stock Market chapter) only invests in companies that meet strong environmental, social, and corporate governance (ESG) standards. In 2017, VFTNX returned 24% while the

S&P 500 returned 22%[11]. The Calvert Large Cap Index (CISIX), another collection of responsibly-managed companies, outperformed the S&P 500 in four of the ten years, while performing almost as well in all the others.

Annual Total Return (%)			
		Sustainable Index Funds	
	S&P 500	Vanguard FTSE Social Index (VFTNX)	Calvert Large Cap Index (CISIX)
2017	21.83	24.19	21.18
2016	11.97	10.34	10.71
2015	1.4	1.3	1.1
2014	13.5	14.4	15.9
2013	32.2	35	37.1
2012	15.9	17.7	17.8
2011	2.1	0.1	0.5
2010	14.8	13.7	14.6
2009	25.9	34.8	35.3
2008	-36.6	-39.7	-42.3

A Quick Tangent on Returns

Given that I just told you could have earned 24% return in a year, I must clarify a few things.

First, 24% returns are not typical. The market grew over 24% in 8 out of the last 30 years. You would have lost money (sometimes up to 40%) in five of the last 30 years, almost as many as it returned above 24%. Not to mention, historical average is *never* predictive of future returns. The stock market is random, we just happen to apply historical averages to it.

Second, your investments may be earning less than you *think* you're

---

[11] Keep in mind, 24% and 22% returns are not typical.

earning. When I asked survey respondents how much they expected to earn investing in the market, many people said 10% per year. (Many respondents had no idea what the return was, but still believed they were maximizing returns this way.)

From 1966-2015, the stock market returned an average 9.7% per year. But since all of us have to invest through funds, there are advisory fees and hidden mutual fund fees that detract from the overall return (see *Fees Kill*, in Investing Primer). Advisory fees plus mutual fund fees average 2% of assets, so if you earned 10% on your $100,000 portfolio this year, you'd have paid $2,000 in fees, reducing your $10,000 in earnings to $8,000, or 8%.

The stock market may have averaged 9.7%, but fees created real returns of 7.7%.

Stock Market Average Returns		
	1966–2015	1966—1981
Average returns	9.70%	5.90%
Adjusted for mutual fund fees and advisory fees	7.70%	3.90%

My final note on returns is: keep in mind, if you lose 50% in one year, you don't have to earn 50% to make your money back. You have to earn 100%. Because math.

Back to Sustainable Funds & Profitability

The latest research reveals that sustainable companies are shattering the myth that doing the right thing isn't profitable. Just the opposite, in fact.

In 2015, Morgan Stanley, a significant player in the financial services world, reviewed over 10,000 open-end mutual funds and found over the previous fifteen years that sustainable funds tended to exhibit slightly higher returns and lower volatility than their traditional counterparts.[ii]

The study also tracked the MSCI KLD 400 Social Index, a collection of 400 stocks screened on environmental, social, and governance (ESG) factors while leaving out industries like alcohol, gambling, tobacco, weapons, and adult entertainment. **This fund's returns were over 100% higher than the S&P 500 from 1990-2015.**[12]

Morningstar, a $1 billion investment research provider, released a report in 2018 titled "Does Investing Sustainably Mean Sacrificing Return?" The report found that of the 20 stock indexes in Morningstar's Global Sustainability Index family, 16 beat their non-sustainable equivalent over their lifespan. The report also highlights that **companies in the sustainable indexes have been "less volatile and possessed of stronger competitive advantages and healthier balance sheets than their non-ESG equivalents."**[iii]

When it comes to the stock market, sustainable investing offers the ability to earn just as much money, if not more. At the same time, sustainable investments often carry much less risk than typical investments, which allows you to feel safer about the money you're counting on.

As the future becomes more resource-constrained—less water, less clean air, and more people demanding more stuff—investors truly have to ask themselves which companies and which investments will be the winners? Will it be the ones polluting that air, or will it be the ones working to clean it up? Your job, as an investor and an engaged citizen, is to ask these questions, too.

Wary of the market?

Only 23% of 18-37 year-olds think the stock market is the best place to put long-term money. Even world-renowned investors believe the next 50 years of stock market won't generate the same kind of returns as the last 50 years.

While many of us have good reason to be afraid of the market, **not investing for the long term could have huge impacts on wealth later in life**. This doesn't mean you have to invest in the market though.

But if you're not invested at all, your money is losing value. Why? Inflation. The cost of stuff—food, rent, transportation—all increase slowly over time. Over the last 10 years, inflation averaged 1.7% per year, meaning if your bank account is only earning 1% your actually *losing*

---

[12] MSCI KLD 400 averaged 10.14% per year, the S&P 500 9.69% (not adjusted for fees or inflation). The 0.5% per year difference compounded to a 100% difference over 15 years.

value.[13]

Not only are you losing money to inflation, you are missing out on the power of compounding. If you're not familiar with compounding, think about a snowball rolling down a hill. The bigger it gets, the more surface area picks up more snow. Eventually, it smashes into the bad guy, but that's not the point. When money compounds, the bigger the balance becomes, the bigger the growth.

So, how can one invest if they don't want to play the market? As you'll see, there are options. For example, Wunder Capital finances large solar energy projects while delivering 7.5% returns to its investors, without the ups and downs of the market. American Homeowner Preservation provides a 10% fixed return, CNote offers a short-term 2.5% savings account, and Pattern Energy Group's (PEGI) stock offers a 9% dividend.

While the stock market returns 20% this year, -40% next year, and 0% the next, fixed-income investments like this are profitable and can be used to compound your money with lower risk.

Concern #2: Does it Actually Create a Positive Impact?

A Chinese saying suggests: "If you want happiness for an hour, take a nap. If you want happiness for a day, go fishing. If you want happiness for a year, inherit a fortune. If you want happiness for a lifetime, help somebody."

Sayings usually stick around for a reason. The latest fMRI brain scans show that *giving* activates the same parts of the brain that are stimulated by food and sex.

End-of-life care providers have distilled the questions people most often asked at the end: *Did I live? Did I love? Did I matter?*

So what do science, a saying, and dying people have in common? Maybe—just maybe—making a difference is key to living a good life.

Yet, the second concern—does sustainable investing actually make a positive impact?—still looms large in our minds. **Can we *actually* make a difference?**

---

[13] If you started sweating at the mention of inflation, don't worry, I've got you covered. There's a primer with the basics of investing in Part 3 of this book

To see if it's possible, we need transparency. The philanthropic world has Charity Navigator, a website with 11 million visitors every year, that details how efficiently and effectively and non-profit organization is run. Some of the organizations in this book can be found there.

Non-profit organizations file Form 990, disclosing their assets, how they are governed, and typically the quantifiable impact they make. Public companies, like the ones in the stock market, must report their financial performance every year and many of the responsible ones create a sustainability or CSR report, too.

Using publicly available knowledge, I created a sample portfolio of do-gooder investments to see what kind of impact one could make.

One person, who invests $100,000 into a sustainable portfolio, has the power to do the following in one year:
- Finance 10 poor women entrepreneurs.
- Reduce 2,000 pounds of coal burned.
- Help install 5 kilowatts of solar energy.
- Support 3 organic farming families.
- Install energy efficient windows in their own home.
- Keep 3 American homeowners in their homes.
- Finance 1 healthy food store in a low-income community.
- Fund the growth of a start-up social enterprise making beautiful products from ocean plastic.[14]
- Bank with a bank that runs on 100% renewable energy and pays their employees a living wage.

This is just one year of impact. Over the next 20 years, this same $100,000 is recycled and reinvested, compounding the impact more than 20 times. How beautiful is that?

Here are a few more ways you could create impact with specific examples from investments in this book:

---

[14] www.dotheincredible.com. No, I am not above self-promotion.

- Lift an 18-year-old single mother out of poverty with an initial $60 loan in Paraguay.
- Help revitalize central Baltimore with investments in artists.
- Finance an early childhood education centers to a community living in poverty.
- Build transition housing in Portland, OR for formerly homeless.
- Lend $7,500 to two organic farmers in Colorado.
- Install thousands of solar panels and wind turbines.
- Invest $250 along with 1,000 others to crowdfund a startup building a $10,000 electric car.
- Bank with a bank funding clean energy or supporting a $15 minimum wage (and that's with zero risk, zero investment involved!)

Concern #3: Utter Confusion

The confusion that comes with investing—virtuous investing nonetheless—is enough to paralyze even the boldest of do-gooders.

But what if, instead standing paralyzed at the edge of a dark forest, we raised up a bright light to see what's there? My humble hope is that this book can be that light.

Sustainable investing is a brave new world, but nothing common sense and research can't handle. This book is designed to be a simple-to-understand guide. It sets the investing options before you like a smorgasbord so you can learn how to choose among these options to build an investment strategy that grows your money while supporting causes you care about.

Throughout, I do my best to be transparent, letting you know when something is good or bad. I also do my tongue-holding-best to not be prescriptive. It's a choose-your-own adventure, not dogma.

Leave behind anything that doesn't make sense.

Ask more questions.

Never stop learning.

One early reader wrote back:

"This book gave me the confidence to reallocate my investments...into a more diverse portfolio of higher impact, higher return investments and the actionable resources to do so immediately."

If you read this book and follow where it leads you, I have no doubt you can cast aside the confusion and truly align your money and your values.

" WHEN ASKED IF I AM
PESSIMISTIC OR OPTIMISTIC
ABOUT THE FUTURE. MY
ANSWER IS ALWAYS THE SAME:
IF YOU LOOK AT THE SCIENCE
ABOUT WHAT IS HAPPENING ON
EARTH AND AREN' T
PESSIMISTIC. YOU DON' T
UNDERSTAND DATA. BUT IF YOU
MEET THE PEOPLE WHO ARE
WORKING TO RESTORE THIS
EARTH AND THE LIVES OF THE
POOR. AND YOU AREN' T
OPTIMISTIC. YOU HAVEN' T GOT
A PULSE. WHAT I SEE
EVERYWHERE IN THE WORLD
ARE ORDINARY PEOPLE WILLING
TO CONFRONT DESPAIR.
POWER. AND INCALCULABLE
ODDS IN ORDER TO RESTORE
SOME SEMBLANCE OF GRACE.
JUSTICE. AND BEAUTY TO THIS
WORLD."

— PAUL HAWKEN

A Time of Great Need

In 1944, 29 reindeer were imported onto St. Matthew Island, a research station, as a backup food source. A few months later, the station was decommissioned and people left the island. With plenty of delicious lichen and no predators, the reindeer did what fat, happy animals do—they proliferated. Thirteen years later, a few researchers returned to find 1,300 still fat, happy, and healthy reindeer. The population boomed to 6,000 six years later, but the large herds had decimated the once bountiful, nutritious lichen and were subsisting on sedge grass. Within three years, thousands of reindeer skeletons littered the island. Only 41 females and one infertile male reindeer remained. The entire population eventually died off.

I have no desire to be a doomsday prophet. Too many already. Fear can be used for motivation, but it's not the world I want to live in. Yet, as Paul Hawken, author of *Ecology of Commerce*, puts it:

"If you look at the science about what is happening on earth and aren't pessimistic you don't understand data."

If the Earth used Facebook, her social media feed might read like this:

"So, here's what's happening in my life right now...."

"Carbon dioxide in my atmosphere is highest its been in millions of years—over 400 parts per million. Not feeling so good. In fact, my temps are up. Oceans are absorbing the excess CO_2, reducing their oxygen levels. 😠"

"Saying goodbye to my loves. 10 species went extinct today (just like yesterday). Super sad to see them go!"[15]

"Thirsty, y'all? The Ogallala Aquifer, one of my largest aquifers lying under 8 U.S. states, is on the verge of depletion. It helps water thousands of acres of crops and millions of people. (Once depleted, it will take 6,000 years to recharge.) Oh well, I've got the time, but do you?"

"Shit's getting scary. 80% of China's underground well water is not safe for drinking or bathing because of heavy pollution[16]. Even in "100% Pure" New Zealand, 60% of rivers and lakes are unfit for swimming."

"I'm officially in Ecological Deficit. Y'all are using 2 times the amount of resources I create every year. Not sure how long I can do on like this…"

"This shit cray! My oceans will contain more plastic than fish by 2050.[iv] A little help, anyone? 😖"

"Been busy around here. Here's what my people are up to…"

"1 billion of my people don't have access to electricity or clean drinking water yet."

---

[15] "Our planet is now in the midst of its sixth mass extinction of plants and animals—the sixth wave of extinctions in the past half-billion years. We're currently experiencing the worst spate of species die-offs since the loss of the dinosaurs 65 million years ago. Although extinction is a natural phenomenon, it occurs at a natural "background" rate of about one to five species per year. Scientists estimate we're now losing species at 1,000 to 10,000 times the background rate, with literally dozens going extinct every day As many as 30 to 50 percent of all species are possibly heading toward extinction by 2050." Center for Biological Diversity.

[16] The Ministry of Water Resources the People's Republic of China

"Shout out to the 821 million home sapiens facing chronic food deprivation. We're trying, y'all!"

"Air pollution is on the rise and helped kill 6.5 million of my people in 2015[v]. Not sure if asking everyone to just take a breath is a good idea anymore. 🤮"

"My people are getting locked up, not rehabilitated. 2.2 million are jailed in the U.S. alone. BTW, the U.S. has 5% of the world's population, but 25% of its prisoners. Was never very good at math, but doesn't add up..."

Even if the Earth doesn't have its own Facebook feed, many of us see daily news in our feeds like this. It can be painful, overwhelming, and sometimes too much to handle.

Picture: Trash collecting in the ocean.

Picture: Air pollution in Mumbai and Delhi, India claimed over 80,000 lives in 2015.

Thankfully, this isn't the only feed.

Incalculable Balance

Right under our very eyes, the Earth is working to maintain an incalculable, yet intricately interwoven balance of life.

Imagine the once-submerged sea beds that have become vast African deserts. Their dust storms carry dead diatoms, or single-celled algae, across the ocean to fertilize the Amazonian rainforest. The Amazon, in turn, produces massive volumes of moisture that condense in the Andes, carrying food down the rivers to our oceans, where algae create the oxygen we need to breathe. One of the many intimate, yet fragile circles of life.

We live inside these circles. When record droughts take their toll on Syrian farmers, radical extremists emerge with cash in return for taking up arms. As oceans absorb more carbon dioxide, the water acidifies and warms, killing off tiny microbes inside coral reefs and wiping out whole fisheries, on which 3 billion people rely for food.

I'll admit, I don't like hearing these findings any more than you. It's like gorging on a big bowl of melancholy soup. And, damn, it needs way more salt. But we have two choices: Starve ourselves and remain blind, or cozy up with the state of the world, even if it's not pretty.

The Golden Rule

In college, my economics professor opened the class with a phrase I'd never forget: "Economic growth is the answer to *everything*." The phrase seared into my spongy, sophomore skull, becoming a motto of sorts. After college, I emerged into the world wearing the rose-colored glassed of *unfettered economic growth*.

Like every buffet, it was too good to be true. As I've traveled the world, it's become clear to me that we can't manage many more years of *unfettered economic growth*. I'm sorry Professor Buckles, but you were wrong.

But here we are. The world is the way it is because we didn't know it could be any different. Now we do.

Don't forget the golden rule: **"He who has the gold makes the rules."**

Over the next 30 years, an epic $30 trillion in North America alone will be passed down from Baby Boomers to Generation X to Millennials.[vi] (Save the complaining about Millennials—they're going to need that money to clean this place up.)

For much of history, the *golden rule* has been brandished by kings, pharaohs, and nefarious industrialists. Times have changed. Even if you consider yourself a 99-percenter, do-gooders by some estimates already collectively hold $20 trillion in wealth, with several trillion more trickling in soon. What rules will you make?

Harnessing the Force

Despite the callous reviews, I loved the *The Last Jedi*. As Luke waxed poetic, sharing how the balance of *The Force* moves through everything, and tips back and forth, I geeked out. I also took notes. George Lucas was hinting at phenomena we rarely pause to observe.

In our less-exciting, yet very real world, we're in the presence of unseen forces, too. In some cases, we can't measure these forces. Yet, many disciplines are hell-bent on computing just how large and persuasive these underlying macro forces are. Economics, for example, measures human behavior and the flow of money to predict what will happen to economic systems. Stocks markets measure how people feel about the economy's prospects. Elections measure the sentiments of the people.

There are two forces we've yet to meaningfully measure—and harness—that could either rescue humanity or let it wander into oblivion. Young Padawan, it's time *you* harnessed the force.

Wealth x Human Values

In many ways, sustainability is like measuring *The Force*. Good vs. evil, yes, but more than that a balance of two powerful measures: Wealth and Human Values.[17]

Sustainability means meeting the needs of the present without compromising future generations' ability to meet their own. This definition implies that to do this we must have some amount of empathy, or caring, for those who come after us. I categorize this as *Human Values*.

At the same time, to move any meaningful needle of sustainability forward, it will require money. We can call this *Wealth*.

Economists' theories typically state that an increase in wealth is good for everyone. I can still see Professor Buckles standing at the base of the auditorium chanting, "Economic growth is the answer to everything." For many generations, a seemingly unlimited Earth made this idea seem plausible. And yet, unbridled growth—devoid of values—has walked us right up to the front door of existential crisis, waiting to ring the doorbell.

But, what if we could pair our *Wealth* with our increasing sense of *Values*?[18]

A simple illustration of four scenarios below shows how aligning *Wealth* and *Values* will lead to a sustainable outcome for us and our planet.

	Wealth	Values	Sustainability
Scenario 1	+	+	+
Scenario 2	+	-	-
Scenario 3	-	+	-
Scenario 4	-	-	-

[17] Yes, Young Padawan, this is your first lesson.
[18] This highly scientific model ascribes traits like compassion, care, selflessness, and non-harming to the measure of *Values*.

In scenarios 2 and 3, each force doesn't have the resources of the other force to drive sustainability. For example, increased *Wealth* without values increases resource extraction, habitat destruction, feelings of selfishness, and, likely war. In scenario 3, *Values* increase, but there is no money or resources to innovate or repair the damage that has been done. Conserving land, building circular economic models, and cleaning the air take time and money.

Scenario 1 illustrates a model where both *Wealth* and *Human Values* increase. Luckily, this is the scenario we find ourselves in. Any objective measure of *Wealth* is on the rise. Our collective *Values* are historically on the rise as well (despite what the news is telling you).

The next step is aligning these two massive forces. This is where you come in, *Padawan*.

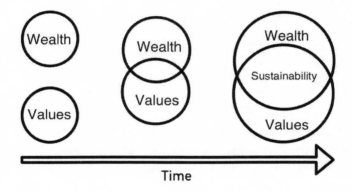

Everything Starts With You

The struggle is real. Some days, I'm fed up. All this typing and working and speaking, yet it feels like I'm trying to lift a box that's secretly glued to the floor. Screw it, I say, as I walk my hope and willpower to the front door and tell them to *get out*. I don't have time for you, I have three seasons of *Narcos* to watch. This is my brain on despair. This is what happens when I think I'm alone, and it's not pretty.

Yet, despite my attempts at self-sabotage, sometimes I'm fortunate to hear the words of my own Mister Miyagi.

"It is easy to believe we are each waves and forget we are also the ocean."[19]

It's easy to forget that we're tethered to everything on this planet and that our thoughts and actions make a difference, no matter how big or small, deep or wide. You may not notice it, but you make up your neighborhood, your state, country, and global society. You are the waves; also the ocean.

When we wake up to this, it's easier to feel more connected to our role in *changing the course of history*. Yep, history.

Float Like a Butterfly

Consider the Butterfly Effect. This phenomenon, popularly known by the phrase "a butterfly flapping its wings in Mexico can cause a typhoon in China," has real roots in meteorological prediction science, and symbolizes the power of small changes that create systemic upheaval.

In 1961, Edward Lorenz ran a numerical computer model to predict the path of a tornado. During the rerun, Lorenz lazily used 0.506 instead of 0.506127 to indicate one of the initial conditions. The result: a *significantly different* weather scenario. In meteorology, this translates to the reality that **a small disturbance in a set of conditions could change the path, delay, accelerate or even prevent the occurrence of a tornado.**

The notion of a deeply interwoven world isn't new. 4,000 years ago in India, questions about the nature of existence began to reveal that each thing *exists* because something—many things—*existed* before it to give rise to it.

Fast forward to quantum mechanics, where *chaos theory* shows how system sensitivity to initial conditions is the largest determinant in an outcome.

The challenges that face our planet and our species are vast, complex, and yet more than ever, it's important to realize the role we play.

---

[19] —Jon J Muth.

Sting Like a Bee

Systems are everywhere. Education *systems*, financial *systems*, food *systems*.

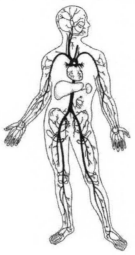

The body is one of the most complex—and miraculous—systems. At its basic living level, it is organized by even smaller, teeny-tiny systems—cells. 37 trillion of them. Cells work together to make organs. Organs operate larger systems, like your circulatory system, nervous system, or reproductive system.

Change one cell and you change the entire system. In fact, your cells are changing every moment. By the time you finish reading this sentence, 50 million of your cells will have died and been replaced by others. You might look the same on the outside, but you are fundamentally different. Change enough cells—say, hitting the gym five days a week—and you'll actually see a difference.

Exhibit A: Change enough cells and you'll see a difference.

But Dwayne Johnson isn't just a pile of juicy muscles. Systems are more than a sum of their parts. They are an *interaction* of their parts, a *synergy* unreplicable by mere parts alone. A single cell can't manage the complexity of an entire body, but together they can run an organ; organs together can manage a complex body.

These 37 trillion individual cells in synergy are so powerful that we've built from basic elements a machine that left our atmosphere, flew through black space, and gently landed on the moon.

But systems are also stubborn.

Like donkeys.

Donkeys don't really move until they want to.

Unless a hornet stings its ass. Then, a donkey will jump a fence with the grace of a gazelle.

Like donkeys, the nature of large systems is simply lumber on, doing what they do. They will not intrinsically initiate change. Some people think systems *resist* change. This isn't quite true. They don't resist change. Until the collective forces acting on the system are large enough, a system won't change. Each little cell in our body is working the daily grind, making energy or filtering blood, not worrying about the system at large. Sound familiar?

Yet, systems *can* and *do* change. How does it happen? Chaos theory suggests large, chaotic systems are highly impacted by small perturbations. Tiny forces deep within a system are the harbingers for change. A single component can trigger change in other components.

A pocket of low pressure air seeds a tornado.

A cancer cell throws a healthy human body into disarray.

A small crack in the snow sets off an avalanche.

A speech triggers a revolution.

So, if a small change can create a chain reaction, **what happens if we can trigger enough small changes in a system?** Can we influence global policy? Energy use? Compassionate systems?

I tell you this because you need to know that we are the hornets that will set fire to the donkey's ass.

" YOU NEVER CHANGE
THINGS BY FIGHTING
THE EXISTING REALITY.

TO CHANGE
SOMETHING. BUILD A
NEW MODEL THAT
MAKES THE EXISTING
MODEL OBSOLETE."

—BUCKMINSTER FULLER

Building a Better Model

Together, we're building a new model. It's the only way to build a world we want to live in. A world we're even more proud of.

F. Scott Fitzgerald said "the test of first-rate intelligence is the ability to hold two opposed ideas in the mind at the same time, and still retain the ability to function."

I propose these: Today's world is amazing, but it also faces existential threats.

Imagine All the People

A few chapters ago, Earth's Facebook feed felt like being tied to an apocalyptic whipping post. Bad human!

Yet, the world benefits daily from everyday people who care. Each day around the world 250,000 people graduate from poverty. 300,000 get electricity for the first time. Another 285,000 get their first access to clean drinking water.[vii]

That's not the end. Deaths from war are the lowest they've been in 500 years. 100 million lives have been saved via vaccinations, better nutrition, and medical care since 1990. Just 40 years ago, more than 50% of adults were illiterate. In 2017, 85% of adults could read. More girls than ever are attending school. Solar power is growing exponentially, and on April 30, 2017 Germany produced 85% of its power from renewables.[viii]

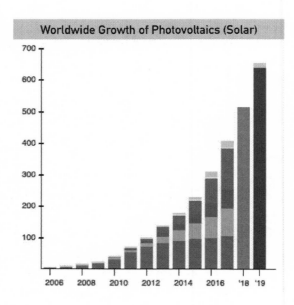

Modern Day Potters

Progress isn't arbitrary. The world has become a safer, healthier place because someone cared. In this case, a lot of someones cared.

We can see deeper into history and further into the future than any other point in human history. We know more about our bipedal ancestors, early civilizations, and the fall of empires than ever before. We have the capabilities of advanced prediction models and exponentially-expanding computing power that allow us to look forward and ask "what if?" with extreme precision.

We are modern day potters, the future a formless blob of clay waiting hopeful on the wheel. It won't be perfect, but with our hands and our tools and our visions of what it can become as guides, we can solve any existential problem in our path.

Sisyphus, Or Not?

We are on the cusp of transformation.

The proverbial boulder has been pushed up the hill. Millions of changemakers and activists and everyday do-gooders have been pushing humankind forward for thousands of years. Ghandi, Mandela, Carson,

Lovins, King, and millions more.

In the stories of ancient Greece, the cruel king Sisyphus was punished to push a boulder up a hill, only to find that it always rolled back down when he got it to the top.

Today, hundreds of millions of people just like you are pushing a massive boulder and we're nearing the top. Will we befall the same fate as Sisyphus?

As you read this:

- A 24-year-old and his team at the Ocean Clean Up are deploying new technology to clean up the oceans. He was 18 when he launched the project.

- A small drone is delivering blood to patients in rural Rwanda.

- AIR-INK is capturing deadly air pollution and turning it into high-quality ink for pens.[20]

Name a challenge. Someone is out there working to solve it.

Humanity is rubbing its bleary eyes as it wakes up to its full potential. The best and the brightest are setting their sights on the existential problems facing our species and our planet.

In the coming chapters, you'll see just how you can take your place alongside the millions of others pushing for a better world. You'll learn about organizations that share your values and how to choose among these options to build an investment strategy that allows you to safely grow your money while supporting causes you care about. And it's easier than you think.

Take OpenInvest, for example. This investment platform lets you opt-out of investing in destructive corporate behaviors with a few clicks. For example, you can tailor your investments by:
- Divesting from dark money (corporate money that shapes policy)
- Divest from carbon emissions
- Divest from deforestation

---

[20] Air pollution was linked to 6.5 million deaths in 2015.

- Divest from gun violence
- Invest in pro-LGBTQ companies
- Invest in companies supporting refugees

The Vision

If we take action, we can create something pretty beautiful. Here's what is possible:

100% clean water.
100% clean air.
100% clean energy.
Equal opportunities no matter where you were born.
Zero unnecessary hunger.
Zero deaths from war.
Thriving ecosystems, balancing all life.

I believe this reality is out there waiting for us.

Are you in?

$10 Billion and Change

Any change you make—a new bank account, a local food company loan, or solar panels soaking up sun—is big change.

Introducing the #DoGooderInvesting Challenge

The #DoGooderInvesting Challenge invites one million do-gooders to make a shift with their money.

When one million people shift just $10,000 each, we will collectively have shifted $10 billion into sustainable and equitable progress. Yes, that's billion with a <u>B</u>!

Some of you will invest your first $100 (very important!), others a $500,000 nest egg. It's all welcome in the #DoGooderInvesting Challenge.

How to Activate

1. Go to www.adrianreif.com/dogoodersguide where you can anonymously submit the amount of money you've shifted.
2. Tell 10 friends about the #DoGooderInvesting Challenge.
3. Sleep easy knowing your money grows with purpose.

Bonus

I want to match you. I don't have $10 billion, but I've pledged 100% of the profits from the sales of this book will be invested in sustainable and equitable organizations—the same ones you'll find in the pages ahead.

Let's do this.

Part 1 Review

- Concerns about profitability, positive impact, and confusion are the biggest hurdles people feel when considering sustainable investing.
- Data shows that sustainable investments are just as profitable as less-sustainable investments—if not slightly more profitable—while often carrying much less risk, allowing investors to feel safer about their money.
- A modest impact portfolio of $100,000 can, in one year:
  - Finance 10 poor women entrepreneurs.
  - Reduce 2,000 pounds of coal burned.
  - Help install 5 kilowatts of solar energy.
  - Support 3 organic farming families.
  - Install energy efficient windows in their own home.
  - Keep 3 American homeowners in their homes.
  - Finance 1 healthy food store in a low-income community.
- Today's world is amazing, but it also faces existential threats.
- System change is driven by tiny forces deep within the system (hint: you).
- We are on the cusp of transformation. You can change the course of history.

In the chapters ahead, you'll learn about organizations you can invest in to create a better world.

" DO THE BEST YOU CAN
UNTIL YOU KNOW
BETTER. THEN WHEN
YOU KNOW BETTER. DO
BETTER."

—MAYA ANGELOU

PART 2

SETTING A COURSE

Finding the Way

On mountain trails, challenging paths are usually lined by cairns—stacks of rocks—to help future travelers find the way. This chapter is a little like that. The ideal of sustainable investing is a super-sized journey and each organization is a tangible signal guiding the way. I hope you'll find these investments fascinating. I sure do. Get ready. You'll soon be a sustainable investing expert.

What's Coming

The upcoming chapters are organized by things you care about. The investing-themed chapters include:

Local Investing
Community Investing and Poverty Alleviation
Diversity, Inclusion, and Equity
Microfinance
Affordable Housing
Renewable Energy
Food System Change
Nature Conservation
A More Sustainable Stock Market
Automated Investing for Do-Gooders
Crowdfunding & Angel Investing in Do-Gooding Companies
Finding a Financial Advisor

And the Bonus Chapter:
Greening Your Home as an Investment

A heads up, Part 2 is chock-full of investment options. Sardine-style. I worried about this book being too *dense*, but I realized my readers are changemakers and do-gooders who are as excited about this stuff as I am.

I want to give you every tool I can to enhance your investing journey.

Because this book was designed to be *the* go-to reference database for the most transformative and profitable investments available to everyday investors,[21] this part will walk you through the investing options. In short, it's like turning the puzzle pieces face up before putting the puzzle together.

Don't worry, you don't have to memorize the list. Or even read every one. Like every choose-your-own-adventure, you can flip to the pages that excite you most.

In Part 3, you'll learn how to choose among these options to build an investment strategy that allows you to safely grow your money while supporting causes you care about.

*While I cover almost every sustainable and ethical investment out there, I left out investments that have marginal positive impact or are very difficult for the everyday investors like us to access.

A Little About the Investments

The investments in this book range in asset class, risk, and target return. For example, returns range from 0.85% to 80%. Asset classes range from guaranteed savings accounts that finance clean energy to moonshot startups building affordable electric cars. You can find investments that fit your needs and desires.

Chapter Review

There is a table at the end of each chapter summarizing key features of each investment. You can use it to quickly find investments that fit your needs. Key features include:

Term — The amount of time you must keep your money in an investment. Some investments, like stock market investments, have a 1 day term (you could sell them same day). Other investments may have 7 year terms, meaning you'll get paid interest each year, but your full principal will be paid back in 7 years.

---

[21] The sustainable investing universe can change rapidly. For the most up-to-date database, join me at: www.adrianreif.com/dogoodersguide for free resources.

Target Return — The amount of financial return that can be expected*
on a yearly basis, if everything goes to plan.

*So, here's the deal. My editors emphatically told me not to include
returns. Returns can change from year to year. And for some investments,
like those in the stock market or in a startup building electric cars, the
potential returns are widely variable. (Like, could-be-big-or-could-lose-
your-entire-investment variable.) Others are as close to guaranteed as the
money under your mattress. I include returns in this book because I want
you to be able to see the general landscape of sustainable investing so you
can orient your investing strategy accordingly. In return, you agree not to
email me and say, "Yo Adrian, where's my 10% return?" Always do your
due diligence before investing.

Minimum Investment — The minimum amount of money you'll need
to invest in a particular investment.

Asset Class — The type of investment, usually indicating a level of risk,
liquidity, and potential returns. Here are the different asset classes I
include:

Cash - Investments like savings accounts or CDs that have low-risk
profiles, and lower expected returns. Some cash investments like savings
accounts can be accessed daily. Others, like renewable energy CDs, may
have terms up to 5 years.

Fixed Return - Like giving someone a loan, a fixed return investment pays
you back a fixed amount every year. You'll receive your initial investment
amount at the end of the term. Fixed return investments are usually low
risk However, the target returns are usually lower, between 1 and 5%,
although a few have returns up to 10%. Fixed return investments can offer
a steady return and money growth that is not linked to a volatile stock
market and may have a place in a long-term portfolio.

Equity - Equity means ownership. Investing in an equity investment
means you are gaining ownership in that organization, usually a company.
For example, when you buy a stock, you own a tiny share of that company

(as a shareholder, you can actually vote on their annual resolutions, including items like "Should we have a climate change strategy?") The most common equities are stocks in the stock market. ETFs invest in stocks, but they are more diversified because they usually own 100+ stocks at a time. Equities have high risk since their return is usually based on how well the company does. Stock market investing has produced yearly returns between -40% and +40%, with some individual companies losing all their value or growing 100% in stock value in a year. The point is: equities can be risky, but diversification can help you manage risk.

Startups - Also known as angel investing, startup investing is investing directly in a young company. Think of startup investing like a social good lottery ticket: you could help fund the next Tesla and earn a big return, or the company could go out of business, meaning you lose all of your investment. Startup investing can be very rewarding, often helping bring about needed innovation, but only invest in startups if you can afford to lose the money. In the Community Investing and Equity Crowdfunding chapters, you'll learn how everyday investors can participate in young, sustainable startups with as little as $100.

Evaluating Investments

Picking investments is very personal. They should fit into your overall investment strategy, which may include liquidity needs (shorter terms), risk preferences, and target returns. Part 3 discusses how to construct your portfolio in detail.

Choosing investments can also be fueled by your values. Some do-gooders are on a mission to create a healthier food system, so they invest with organizations like RSF who lend to food system entrepreneurs. The financial return is low, but the positive impact is high. I invite you to evaluate each investment on its risk, terms, and target returns, but also consider the company's experience, leadership, and the positive impact it makes on the world.

Let's get started.

Local Investing

The Local Movement has infected millions of people as a yin to globalization's yang.

In 2018, Berkeleyside—a local news website for Berkeley and East Bay—raised *$1 million dollars* **in investment from its readers** instead of reaching out to large investment firms or other media companies, so it could keep reporting locally and independently.

Local investing is powerful: it can lift up communities left behind by globalization, connect neighbors in meaningful ways, and even serve as a decentralized way to solve problems or unmet needs. Investments are wide-ranging and increasingly creative. In Chicago, Affordable Energy Services provides renewable energy to low-income neighborhoods. In Arlington, OR, a community wind farm raised money from its neighbors. And in many communities, a credit union serves its customers first, not its shareholders.

Let's see how communities are lifting themselves up and how you can find local investments.

Investments Ahead

Local Banking | How to ensure your checking and savings accounts are doing more for your community.

CuttingEdgeX | an online platform where you can search for local companies raising capital from their community.

Investibule | A search engine to find people and companies raising funds. Search by state, women-owned businesses, people of color, and more.

Slow Money | A non-profit with local investment chapters around the world aspiring to bring money back down to Earth.

Adrian's Aside: On Community

A cul-de-sac where I'd built dirt jumps in backyards for our bikes. A calculus teacher who saw more in me than I could. A Little League coach whose disciplinarian style I'm far more grateful for now. My first company was borne by my community, a feeling of grace I'll never forget.

Our communities shape us.

11,000 years ago our ancestors lived in small bands—a dozen or so people. Tight bonds and reciprocity meant the difference between survival or death. Community was essential.

Today, globalization makes it possible to survive in isolation. You don't need to know which person in your tribe grows potatoes, sews clothes, or knows the path to the river. Globalization is a beautiful thing, but it has cost us a deep human need: *connection.*

We outsourced too much, for too long. We forgot how to grow food. We gave our money to guys in suits and let them run amok. Globalization's efficiencies came with a price.

Yet, people around the world are banding together to resurrect communities left behind. The Local Movement has sprung up as a yin to globalization's faceless yang.

Take the swell in farmers' markets for example. We yearn for connection more than ever and a farmers market offers a small recompense. When I walk through the cozy farmers' market in my small mountain town on Saturday mornings, I smell more than roasted chilies in the air. I smell connection.

The same goes for farmers' markets in Omaha, Nebraska and Brooklyn, New York.

One of my mentors said that acts like farmers markets are born from a desire to grow closer. He believes we need a "deeper materialism" to cope with the modern world. Deeper materialism is the idea that our *material* world, not just our spiritual world, can be sacred. Indeed, what if we worshipped our food and our water, and, heck even our TVs? We'd have a deeper connections to all the things in our lives. Like a photo on an altar, we'd cherish them and protect them, not pollute them or toss them into massive toxic piles.

Even more, community might be essential to life. Okinawa, a Japanese island, has one of the highest concentrations of centenarians — people over

100 years old — on the planet. Research popularized by the book *Blue Zones*, determined that "moais", or social support groups, are critical to an individual's well-being and longevity.[22]

On the flip side, globalization will march on. Humans have been globalizing since we hopped out of trees. The caravans that traveled the Silk Road brought salt from Africa to the Far East and returned with silk, spices, and gunpowder. Today, the Silk Road is a paved interstate going from the eastern Chinese seaboard to downtown Hamburg, Germany.

The planet has always been smaller than we think. While China funds roads in Africa, European companies buy up Great-American breweries. We don't pause to lament as one of the world's 7,000 languages dies every 9 days.

As globalization marches on, it's up to us to choose what we keep and what we leave behind. I believe community and connection are keepers. The good news is that our money can engender healthier communities and stronger connections.

---

[22] Moai means "meeting for a common purpose" in Japanese.

CuttingEdgeX

CuttingEdgeX helps you find Direct Public Offerings (DPOs), allowing you to invest directly in local companies you care about.

DPOs are like IPOs for smaller companies. A company can raise money by selling shares directly to the public (you) without the high costs of investment banks.

Examples

In 2018, Urban Greens Food Co-op a local-focused healthy food store in Providence, Rhode Island raised $575,000 from 120 local investors. The money helped Urban Greens become community-owned, source more local, healthy foods, while paying their investors 2% interest.

In California, Sonoma West Publishers reinvented small town newspaper ownership by becoming the first print newspaper group in the U.S. to invite its readers to become active shareholders, offering a 3% dividend.

Mr. Sparkle Window Washers in the East Bay raised capital from local investors while offering a 5% interest dividend.

Investibule

Investibule.co provides a searchable database for small companies raising money from everyday investors. Unique to Investibule is the ability to search by state, industry, or even values, like:

- Environmental Impact
- Owners of Color
- Women-Owned
- Benefit Corporations

Previous investments listed on Investibule range from a community wind farm in Arlington, Oregon to Affordable Energy Services, a renewable energy provider for low-income neighborhoods in Chicago.

Slow Money

Founded in 2019, Slow Money has moved $73 million through local chapters into 752 local and organic food enterprises.

In a world of collateralized debt obligations, hedge funds, and other questionable investments, Slow Money is bringing money back down to Earth. While your life might feel like it is speeding up, the Slow Movement is here to help slow it down. Slow food. Slow parenting. Slow travel. Slow fashion. Even Slow sex (look it up!)

Examples

In New York, the Slow Money NYC chapter hosts Jeffersonian Dinners, plated with inspired dialogue, while helping to spur food investment in the New York area foodshed.

A Slow Money chapter in Lawrence, Kansas, loaned $45,000 to Jackie to expand her Animal Welfare Approved lamb products into 15 states.

In Carbondale, Colorado, organic farmers Harper and Christian received a $7,500 loan to help them purchase materials for a mobile walk-in cooler and drip-irrigation system.

Slow Money has also pioneered SOIL—Slow Opportunities for Investing Locally. When you become a SOIL member, you can vote on where the money is loaned. SOIL helped companies like Re:Vision launch Denver's first grocery store that is owned by a community living in a food desert.

To participate, go to Slow Money's website and find a group near you. Investment terms are investment dependent and can range from 0%-5% fixed return loans or equity investments.

Slow Money Principles

1. We must bring money back down to earth.
2. There is such a thing as money that is too fast, companies that are too big, finance that is too complex. Therefore, we must slow our money down — not all of it, of course, but enough to matter.
3. The 20th Century was the era of Buy Low/Sell High and Wealth Now/Philanthropy Later—what one venture capitalist called "the largest legal accumulation of wealth in history." The 21st Century will be the era of nurture capital, built around principles of carrying capacity, care of the commons, sense of place, diversity and nonviolence.
4. We must learn to invest as if food, farms and fertility mattered. We must connect investors to the places where they live, creating healthy relationships and new sources of capital for small food enterprises.
5. Let us celebrate the new generation of entrepreneurs, consumers and investors who are showing the way from Making A Killing to Making a Living.
6. Paul Newman said, "I just happen to think that in life we need to be a little like the farmer who puts back into the soil what he takes out." Recognizing the wisdom of these words, let us begin rebuilding our economy from the ground up, asking:
    *   What would the world be like if we invested 50% of our assets within 50 miles of where we live?
    *   What if there were a new generation of companies that gave away 50% of their profits?
    *   What if there were 50% more organic matter in our soil 50 years from now?

Local Banking

Banking locally is one of the easiest ways to make a difference in your community. Community banks and credit unions prefer to make loans to local businesses and families, not hedge funds. This money stays in your community, supports places you actually use, and has greater oversight.

Find a Local Bank Fast

Lucky for us, the amazing folks at Green America built a national database where you can search and find a local bank, credit union, or even local credit cards.

Search "Green America Break Up With Your Mega Bank" (or go to www.adrianreif.com/dogoodersguide to find the link).

Local Investing—Review

Investing in your local community can uplift your community, create meaningful connection, while offering viable investment options that create impact.

- The Local Movement—including Local Investing—is growing. Several sites can help you quickly find investments in your area, or by certain values, like women-owned companies.
- Slow Money's nationwide chapters connect their members with local food companies, helping support a healthy and connected food system.
- Communities across the country are funding their very own healthy grocery stores, newspapers, news sites, and renewable energy providers.
- Local banking is an easy way to circulating money in your community, not hedge funds.

Investment	Min. Investment	Target Return	Term
CuttingEdgeX	$250	1-6%	1-7 yrs
Investibule	$150	0-100%	1-10 years
Slow Money	$250	0-2%	5-10 years
Local Banking	$5	0-2%	All

Investing in Communities & Poverty Alleviation

Of the 39 million Americans living in poverty, it is estimated that 33% of those people are children.

Regardless the cause of poverty, the length of time a child spends in poverty greatly reduces their achievement as adults.[ix] We know that communities experiencing poverty don't attract good schools, healthy food stores, or high-quality jobs.

Investing in communities can change this. In this chapter, you'll see investments that can help you grow your money while investing in under-resourced communities, minority entrepreneurs, and job creation.

Investments Ahead

Reinvestment Fund | This fund brings early childhood education, high-quality grocery stores, affordable housing, and health centers to low-income communities.

CNote | A high-interest (2.75%) savings account that invests primarily in women and minority-led businesses.

Neighborly | Neighborly helps you fund schools, libraries, parks, and more through municipal bonds.

Calvert Community Investment Note | Invest in affordable housing and job creation, especially among women and Native peoples, through Calvert's one-click Community Investment Note.

Reinvestment Fund

Reinvestment Fund is catalyzing change in low-income communities.

They use data and policy change to target the most inequitable challenges, with results that show investment in low-income communities produce big outcomes.

Reinvestment Fund invests in:
- Early childhood education
- High-quality grocery stores
- Affordable housing
- Health centers
- Artists

Investing in Artists for Poverty Alleviation

Data from Philadelphia found that **artists' networks generate social and economic spillover effects, including positive relationships with poverty reduction (without social displacement), improved child welfare, fewer cases of ethnic and racial harassment, and lower rates of chronic illness.**

Reinvestment Fund is using this data to invest in artists through community projects in Central Baltimore through the Central Baltimore Future Fund, a $10 million loan initiative.

Impact on Re-emerging Communities

Reinvestment Fund's impact is staggering:
- 22,180 homes financed
- 18.4 million square feet of commercial space created
- 77,895 jobs created
- 169 grocery stores and healthy food outlets
- 100% repayment since 1985

The offering is a note with a fixed return.

Term	Interest Rates:	Min. Investment
3-4 year	1.75%	$1,000
5-6 year	2.25%	
7-9 year	2.75%	
10-14 year	3.5%	
15 year	4.5%	

CNote

CNote offers a high-interest (2.75% at time of writing) savings account while investing in historically disenfranchised entrepreneurs and business owners.

For every $1,000 invested with CNote, one underserved entrepreneur is impacted with a loan for their business. CNote invests in a network of Community Development Finance Institutions (CDFIs for short) that operate locally and provide loans to business owners who usually don't qualify—typically women and minority-led businesses.

The return that CNote offers makes it a great place to park long-term cash. Unlike a regular savings account, you can only access your money every 3 months. This allows CNote to lend fluidly.

Neighborly

Neighborly helps you find *municipal bonds*—loans made to cities and school districts—that fund schools, libraries, parks, and more.

On top of investing in community services, municipal bonds are great investment vehicles for two reasons: 1) The income earned is *tax-free*. High income earners will often invest in municipal bonds to help manage taxes. 2) Muni bonds are less volatile and have higher repayment rates than corporate bonds (which your stocks and bonds portfolio likely owns).

Examples

The Piedmont, CA Unified School District offered bonds raise money to make school improvements including seismic retrofitting. The bond pays a 4.4% interest rate[23].

Term: 1 year - 20 year options
Return: 1% - 4.5%
Minimum Investment: $1,000 - $5,000

Calvert Community Investment Note

Calvert Impact Capital is an established non-profit investment firm using its investments to make the world more equitable and sustainable.

Examples: Helping Homeless Veterans

Calvert's Community Investment Note (CCIN) invests in organizations like REACH Community Development Inc., an affordable housing developer in Portland, Oregon. REACH operates an apartment building in downtown Portland where 20% of the units—42 apartments—are set aside for formerly homeless Veterans referred by the VA. A VA case manager is also on site 20 hours per week to coach these Veterans through financial or life challenges.

Housing is just one example. Calvert also invests in organizations supporting people over age 50, women's equity around the world, Native American communities, renewable energy, sustainable agriculture, and education.

---

[23] This is the Tax Equivalent Yield, meaning when the savings on taxes is included, you earn 4.4%.

Impact Overview

Since 1995, Calvert's Community Invest Note has created tangible impact:

- 5,287 affordable housing units created or preserved
- 3,715 jobs created or preserved
- 120,000 microfinance customers served
- 4,500+ investors like you
- 100% repayment rate

The investment is a note with a fixed return.

Term and Interest Rate
1 year – 1%
3 year – 1.5%
5 year – 2%
10 year – 3%
15 year – 4%

Minimum investment: $20 online through Vested.org; $1,000 through a brokerage account (like Schwab or TD Ameritrade) or direct with Calvert.

Investing in Communities & Poverty Alleviation—Review

With proven results, investing in communities for education, poverty alleviation, and job creation can lift up others while providing steady returns.

- Thirty-three percent of the 39 million Americans in poverty are children. Focused investments can break the cycle of poverty and help these children become high-achieving adults.
- Artists' networks generate positive social and economic effects, including poverty reduction. This is why Reinvestment Fund invests in artists through revitalization projects.
- A $1,000 in savings can impact one minority entrepreneur with a simple high-interest savings account like CNote.
- Municipal bonds help build schools, libraries and more, and offer tax-free income.

Investment	Min. Investment	Target Return	Term
Reinvestment Fund	$1,000	1.75-4.5%	3-15 years
CNote	$1	2.75%	3 months
Neighborly	$1,000	1-4.5%	1-20 years
Calvert Community Investment Note	$20 / $1,000	1-4%	1-15 years

Diversity, Inclusion, & Equity Investing

It takes a lot to throw a good party. It's been said that Diversity invites you to the party, Inclusion invites you to dance, and Equity offers enough space in the room for guests to host their own parties. While not every party thrower makes these efforts, we're quickly moving toward a more compassionate and accepting world. That doesn't mean we can't do better. Everyone deserves an opportunity to live their best life.

Diversity, inclusion, and equity investing is a growing focus for many folks, especially foundations and family offices who use their investments to build a better world. However, this type of values investing is also making its way into the mainstream, helping everyday investors like you contribute to a world that accepts people regardless of skin color, gender, non-gender, background, age, or religion.

Professional investors are also beginning to focus on diversity, inclusion, and equity metrics because it is clear they point to improved performance in companies. A McKinsey report that studied 366 public companies in the U.S., Canada, Latin America, and the U.K. found that companies in the top quartile for gender or racial and ethnic diversity are more likely to have financial returns above their national industry medians. Companies in the bottom quartile in these dimensions are statistically less likely to achieve above-average returns.[x]

While many investments in this book contribute to advancing diversity, inclusion, and equity as side effects, let's take a look at how you can choose investments that specifically target diversity, equity, and inclusion.

Investments Ahead

Stock Market | Several ETFs and investments platforms focus in on companies that lead the advancement of diversity, which according to McKinsey's research, gives them a competitive financial advantage compared to industry peers.

Community Investing | Organizations like Reinvestment Fund, American Homeowner Preservation, and Calvert Community Investment Note.

Microfinance | Microfinance takes aim at underserved entrepreneurs around the world. Sixty-eight percent of microfinance customers are women (and, surprise, these women tend to be more reliable at paying back loans).

Angel Investing | Several platforms allow you to find and invest directly in startups and operational businesses raising capital with search tags like women-owned, veteran, minority-owned, and people of color.

Stock Market

Wall Street is taking notice of the rise in demands for equitable investments, and many companies are stepping up to the plate. The following investment options—while not perfect—can help you add a diversity lens to your portfolio.

ETFs & Mutual Funds

The **SPDR® SSGA Gender Diversity ETF (SHE)** seeks to track the performance of companies that are leaders in advancing women through gender diversity on their board of directors and in management. It has a modest 0.20% expense ratio.

The other fund is **PAX Ellevate Global Women's Leadership (PXWEX),** a mutual fund that invests in the highest rated companies in the world for advancing women via their boards and in executive management. While this mutual fund ranks a bit higher on sustainability, its 0.81% expense ratio[24] makes it a tough sell.

OpenInvest

OpenInvest is an investment platform—sign up, transfer money, and it helps you manage stock market investments with low fees and the ability to choose value themes you care about. One of their selection processes includes *Invest in Pro-LGBTQ Companies* and *Invest in Women in the Workplace*, two ways to reward companies advancing diversity and inclusion.

Community Investing

These organizations discussed throughout the book directly impact people who've been historically disenfranchised, often help break cycles of poverty and provide jobs, education, and access to business funds for women and minority entrepreneurs.

---

[24] Expense ratios are discussed at length in the *A More Sustainable Stock Market* chapter.

Reinvestment Fund

This loan fund brings early childhood education, high-quality grocery stores, affordable housing, and health centers to low-income communities.

CNote

A high-interest (2.75%) savings account that invests primarily in women and minority-led businesses.

American Homeowner Preservation (AHP)

AHP buys up homes that banks are foreclosing on and then works to keep homeowners in their homes, helping keep low-income populations in their homes.

Calvert Community Investment Note

Calvert's easy-to-invest-in loan fund invests in affordable housing and job creation, especially among women and Native peoples.

Microfinance

The microfinance chapter features several organizations like Kiva, Zidisha, and Working Capital for Community Needs (WCCN) that primarily invest in women entrepreneurs around the world. Given that 70% of the world's poor are women, access to capital is a significant driver in uplifting women, family planning, and normalizing women's place in the world. Platforms like Kiva, which makes micro-loans, are neat because you can see the entrepreneur or student you are lending to.

Angel Investing

If you want to invest directly in companies owned by women, people of color, and veterans, several sites mentioned throughout the book can help you find and evaluate these investments.

Investibule, CuttingEdgeX, and Republic Crowdfunding are three platforms that can help you find investments that fit your diversity-focused needs.

Diversity, Inclusion, & Equity Investing—Review

Many investors are seeking out investments that reflect their desire to see a more just, diverse, and equitable world. While not commonplace, the investment world *is* taking notice.

- Stock market ETFs (like SHE) allow you to invest in the top companies promoting women through board seats and executive management.
- Many community investment funds work to bring education, healthy foods, jobs, and affordable housing to low-income communities, often breaking cycles of poverty and lifting up the most disenfranchised.
- Microfinance customers are 68% women. You can help finance these entrepreneurs through the microfinance organizations featured in this book.
- Angel investing gives you the opportunity to invest directly in diversely-owned businesses, with several platforms featuring search options with diversity metrics.

Investment	Min. Investment	Target Return	Term
Reinvestment Fund	$1,000	1.75-4.5%	3-15 years
CNote	$1	2.75%	3 months
Calvert Community Investment Note	$20 / $1,000	1-4%	1-15 years
Working Capital for Community Needs	$1,000	2%-4%	2 years
Kiva	$25	0%	1 year
Envest (accredited investors)	$25,000	5-6%	2-4 years
Zidisha	$1	0%	1 year
CuttingEdgeX	$250	1-6%	1-7 years
Investibule	$150	0-100%	1-10+ years
Republic	$150	0-100%	5+ years
SPDR Gender Diversity ETF (SHE)	$100	13% since inception (pays 1.8% dividend)	3 days
Pax Ellevate Global Women's Leadership (PXWEX)	$1,000	6.9% since inception (pays a 1.77% dividend)	3 days
OpenInvest (See options to invest in Pro-LGBTQ and Pro-women companies)	$100	Variable, market like returns	3 days

Microfinance

In Tegucigalpa, Honduras Alba Aguilera sells chicken, potatoes, squash, salad, and plantains. In 2012, Alba used up her savings to pay for her brother and nephew's funeral after they were killed. She also began caring for her brother's wife.

Instead of closing her business, Alba borrowed $212 from ASHETFIN, a microfinance organization, to keep her business going. When she paid that loan back, she took out a bigger one. Four years later, Alba's fifth loan had grown to $1,100, allowing her to grow her business yet again. The last loan allowed Alba to purchase a water tank.

While we expect nothing less than 24/7 access to clean water, Alba's water only comes on intermittently, sometimes only once per day. Before buying the tank, Alba would scramble to capture the water in stray buckets, pails, and bottles so she would have enough to wash and prep the food she sells. The new water tank allows Alba to store the water when it comes and focus the rest of her time on her business and family, not filling bottles.

Alba Aguilera, a microfinance customer.

This is microfinance.

The **secret that most people don't know is that Alba's loans came from people like you.**

Financing Equity

> **"Nothing is wrong with the poor. They're as good as anybody else. They're as active as anybody else. They're as creative as anybody else. They're as smart as anybody else. Poverty is not created by the poor people."**
>
> **– Muhammad Yunus**

You may have experienced microfinance when you were younger. A dollar here, five bucks there, handed over by a parent hoping you'd save, but knowing you'd buy sour warheads and see how many you could put in your mouth at once.

While you may not have called it "access to capital" when you were five years old, money is essential in the global advancement toward equity. Yet, banks around the world have historically restrained lending to poor people. For one, the fees to make a $25 loan weren't worth it. And the common conception was *how could poor people pay back a loan?!*

In the 1960s a Bangladeshi named Muhammad Yunus finished his PhD in Economic Development at Vanderbilt University.[25] Back in Bangladesh, he tested his ideas and made loans to *groups* of poor women. His "microcredit" idea became the Grameen Bank.

Several decades later, microfinance has unlocked billions of dollars once inaccessible by poor people. It's been responsible for lifting people out of poverty, building a middle class in countries without one, and ushers our world toward or more fair, just, and equitable one.

Microfinance is responsible for $10 billion of investment around the world, yet most everyday investors are unaware of it. ResponsAbility, a Swiss investment firm, manages a portfolio of about $2 billion in microfinance investments around the world, but unless you are a ultra-wealthy investor, hedge fund, or bank, you cannot access their offerings.

---

[25] My alma mater! *Go Dores!*

How Does Microfinance Work?

Microfinance institutions are banks that serve very low-income populations. Until microfinance, poor people did not have access to credit.

The loans are small. In the early days, loans were usually a few dollars. Today, they range from $20 up to $1,000 for repeat borrowers. Typically, loans are made to a group of people, with peer accountability a key foundation of high payback rates.

Borrowers have a purpose for the loan and pay it back with interest. They could use it to buy inventory for their micro-business, say reselling Coca-Cola or fruit at the market; pay for a child's tuition; buy a taxi car or rickshaw; or buy a pig to raise for food and income. These are just a few examples.

Thanks to several pioneering organizations, you can get in on the action. Here are organizations that allow the everyday investor like you join the microfinance movement.

Investments Ahead

Working Capital for Community Needs (WCCN) | A non-profit that lends money to the working poor, like Alba. They focus on farmers, cooperatives, and small business owners in Latin America.

Envest | Envest targets the most marginalized populations by lending to Tier 3 microfinance organizations, generally the smallest (and riskiest). Envest allows accredited investors to earn a generous 5% return while creating access to capital.

Kiva | A non-profit with a killer website that allows you to find borrowers in 80+ countries. These folks are usually growing their businesses, buying livestock, or paying school fees. I've made loans to women in Pakistan, Cambodia, and Ecuador over the years.

Zidisha | Zidisha removes middlemen like microfinance institutions and allows you to lend directly to borrowers—primarily in Africa—through a cellphone.

Adrian's Aside: The Power of Microfinance

When Muhammad Yunus received the Nobel Peace Prize in 2006, there to accept the award with him was Mosammat Taslima Begum, a Grameen bank customer who used her first $20 loan in 1992 to buy a goat. Fourteen years later, Mosammat ran a small mango orchard, a fish pond and owned a rickshaw for transport operated by her husband—and was one of the Grameen Bank's nine elected board members.

Since its inception in 1983, the Grameen Bank—the first microfinance bank, founded by Yunus—has lent $16 billion to 8 million members.[xi] Over 95% are women. Check this out: The Grameen Bank is 95% owned by the local poor and 5% by the government.

Microfinance was spurred by Yunus's belief that credit is a human right. It can give the people living in poverty means to grow their income and opportunities.

In 2003, the Grameen Bank took another radical step. A new program began distributing interest free loans to "beggars" in Bangladesh. The loans were $1.50. Yes, *one dollar and fifty cents.* The payback period was arbitrarily long and the borrower is covered under life insurance free of cost.

Thanks to this experiment over 16,000 "beggars" have left begging.

The bank has also expanded into collateral-free housing and higher education loans. It serves 81,000 villages in Bangladesh. The Grameen Foundation supports other microfinance institutions in over 27 countries.

Microfinance Faces Criticism

Despite my pollyanna nature, microfinance has faced its detractors. The interest rates charged by some microfinance institutions are steep[26], especially compared to what we are used to seeing with large, established banks.

While this is true, the high interest rates are necessary to pay back several levels of lenders and attract capital from investors like you. Zidisha and Kiva are non-profits and emerged to offer lower rates, but still rely on donations to stay in business.

As an entrepreneur, I've reflected on microfinance. When I started my

---

[26] Though payday lenders in the U.S. are worse.

third company I used a $1,000 in savings to get it off the ground. But as it grew, I needed more money to buy peanuts and coconut, machines, and packaging.

I needed more money, but the business was still so small that banks weren't interested. As luck would have it, my middle-class network likely opened avenues that don't exist for low-income people around the world. I borrowed a small amount of seed capital from family and friends, which kept the business growing. As I reflect on this privilege, I can't fathom the challenge of being a poor farmer trying to make their way up in a developing country.

I've seen microfinance working on the ground in Haiti, Guatemala, China, Mongolia, and Nepal. It changes lives. While it may not be a miracle cure to what ails us, I believe it moves us one step closer to a collective ideal: opportunity. Indeed, I put my money where my mouth is and lend money through organizations like Kiva.

In 2007, I had the privilege of hearing Muhammad Yunus speak as he returned to Vanderbilt to address my graduating class. He said:

> **"The world cannot remain the way it is. It's our Job — your job — to create the world that we want to live in. ... Nobody should be a poor person in that world. There's no need to be."**

I'll toss a cap to that!

Working Capital for Community Needs

Founded in the 1980s to serve economies devastated by war and conflict in Latin America, Working Capital for Community Needs (WCCN), lends money to very low-income Latin American entrepreneurs. They serve 30,000 people each year and have invested $110 million in Latin America since 1991.

Impact Snapshot:

Here's a quick look at some of the impacts WCCN has made:

- Serve 30,000 people each year with loans
- $110 million invested in Latin America since 1991
- $11.8 million currently deployed in Latin America[27]
- 100% repayment rate to investors for 25 years

The investment is a note with a fixed return.

Terms and Target Return:
$1,000 - $14,999; 2 years at 2% or 4 years at 3%
$15,000 - $49,999; 2 years at 3% or 4 years at 3.5%
$50,000 and up; 2 years at 3.5% or 4 years at 4%

Minimum Investment: $1,000

Envest[28]

Envest is a microfinance cooperative that targets marginalized populations by lending to small Tier 3 microfinance institutions. Founded in 2012, the organization has lending partners in ten countries and has loaned money to maize farmers in Zimbabwe, a furniture maker in Nicaragua, and a group of women who became fish brokers and equal partners in their households.

Envest offers both equity investment in their cooperative with a 5-6% return depending on performance and a debt offering with a 4% fixed return. *This investment is only open to accredited investors.

Term: 2-4 years
Targeted Return: 4-6%
Minimum Investment: $25,000

---

[27] As of June 2016.
[28] Accredited investors only

Kiva

Kiva is a non-profit organization that envisions a world where the poor hold the power to create opportunity for themselves and alleviate poverty. Through Kiva you can invest in micro-loans all over the world for as little as $25. While you do not earn a return when investing with Kiva—you simply get paid back—they are featured here because of the impact of what they do.[29]

Impact Snapshot:

- $940 million loaned from people like you since 2005
- 2.2 million borrowers in 82 countries
- 100% of every dollar you lend goes to funding loans
- 97% repayment rate
- You choose who you loan to

Kiva U.S.

Kiva also allows you to lend to financially excluded and socially impactful entrepreneurs in the U.S. making a difference in their community. The loans are 1-3 year loans at 0% interest to the borrowers.

Zidisha

Zidisha is a non-profit with an innovative approach to microfinance that cuts out middlemen, like banks, and allows you to make 0% interest loans. Similar to Kiva, Zidisha does not pay you a return, but you do receive your principal.

Through mobile technology, Zidisha can make loans in Ghana, Indonesia, Kenya, Mexico, Nigeria and Zambia. Since they launched in 2008, Zidisha has loaned over $16 million to 237,000 borrowers.

Through Zidisha.org you can provide credit directly to people around

---

[29] Since 2005, I've made 12 loans to people in Mongolia, Kenya, Guatemala, Pakistan, and more. I've been paid back 100% of the time and when I do, I simply relend the money.

the world with as little as $1. You receive 0% interest and are typically paid back in 1-3 years. A $50 loan will be recycled into $750 worth of loans over 5 years.

"When you hold the world in your palm and inspect it only from a bird's eye view, you tend to become arrogant, you do not realize things become blurred when viewed from an enormous distance. I opted instead for the 'worms eye view'. The poor taught me an entirely new economics. I learned about the problems they face from their own perspective."

– Muhammad Yunus

Microfinance—Review

Microfinance institutions lend money to low-income people and entrepreneurs around the world. Traditionally, these financially marginalized people didn't have access to capital. There's still a demand of about $500 billion in loans that is unmet.

- Since 1983, Grameen Bank has pioneered microfinance, lending $16 billion to 8 million people. It is 95% owned by the communities it invests in.
- Microfinance was spurred by Muhammad Yunus's belief that credit is a human right.
- Working Capital for Community Needs and Envest Microfinance offer profitable returns for investors.
- Kiva and Zidisha can help you make 0% interest loans to entrepreneurs around the world.

Investment	Min. Investment	Target Return	Term
Working Capital for Community Needs	$1,000	2%-4%	2 years
Kiva and Zidisha	$1-$25	0%	1 year
Envest Microfinance	$25,000	5-6%	2-4 years

Affordable Housing

What would it feel like living in a world where you know that every person who wants it has a roof over their head each night?

Some might say it's impossible, but the investments in the pages ahead will make you think differently.

What's At Stake

The challenge is this: the housing market—which no doubt, many of us have benefitted from over the years—treats housing like a commodity, a precious resource available to the highest bidder.

In a world that values providing core human needs to everyone who wants it, market-based housing is a clear failure.

Indeed, you only have to look around. Every major metro area is in a panic over affordable housing. Seattle, Portland, Denver, SF, NYC. Even smaller cities are feeling the pain. The tiny, tight-knit mountain town where I live is facing a serious housing crunch. Home prices have surged, putting even rentals out of the range of many blue-collar and service industry workers that the town depends on.

Right now in the U.S. there is a shortage of 7.4 million affordable rental homes available to extremely low income (ELI) renter[30] households.[31] This does not include homeless needs.

In Austin, Texas, the non-profit Foundation Communities has waitlists at all 19 of its affordable housing buildings. "Waitlists are the longest they've ever been for us. It's hard to keep up with the need," shares Foundation's Alyah Khan.

Federal and state governments are the prime provider of funds for affordable housing, but those budgets have been steadily dropping.

---

[30] ELI is classified as at or below the Poverty Guideline or below 30% of Area Median Income (AMI).

[31] The Gap: A Shortage of Affordable Homes. National Low Income Housing Coalition.

One challenge is a longstanding belief that politicians can fix this mess. But what if we could be part of the solution?

Become the Solution

In the U.S. we invest more money in social media startups than we do in affordable housing. What if our hackers and visionaries turned their attention to this pressing need instead? Hundreds of organizations are already doing that, bringing much needed innovation. Now, with unique investment models, there are possibilities to attract billions of dollars of everyday investor capital while paying a return.

Let's do this. If not for its sheer decency, then for the simple fact that it is possible.

Investments Ahead

American Homeowner Preservation | An investment fund that buys distressed mortgages and keeps homeowners in their homes instead of kicking them out.

Guerrilla Development | A developer in Portland that has crowdsourced investment for some of their housing projects, including *Jolene's First Cousin*[32], a building with transition housing for the formerly homeless.

Enterprise Community Partners | An affordable housing financier that has helped build or renovate 100,000 affordable homes, often including support services for folks transitioning from homelessness.

Small Change | A real estate investing platform that let's you invest in real estate projects that make cities better.

Affordable Homes of South Texas | A builder that serves people under 80% of area median income with 0% mortgages and high-quality, Energy Star Certified homes.

---

[32] What a name. In typical Portland fashion, of course.

Adrian's Aside: The Worst of Humanity and the Best of Humanity in 48 Hours

In 2007, I spent two days living on the streets of D.C. I Thankfully, it was by choice. I turned in everything I owned except a garbage bag filled with a blanket and the clothes on my back.

Eleven college classmates and I opted for an atypical Spring Break and signed up for the Urban Plunge, an experiment through the National Coalition for the Homeless that develops actual empathy for what it's like to live on the streets. *How can we actually understand homelessness fully unless we've experienced it ourselves?*

In 48 hours, I experienced the best of humanity, and the worst of it.

The Plunge began at NCH's small office, where my peers and I handed over cell phones, money, and other "essentials." I stuffed a jacket and a blanket into a black garbage bag and swung it over my shoulder as I headed out the door.

I hit the streets consumed with fear, like a head first dive first into the deep end without knowing how to swim. We were encouraged to get the full experience. I rummaged through garbage cans searching for something useful, only finding embarrassment as bystanders watched. As I held a cardboard sign on street corners asking for money, my face flushed red. Thousands walked past. A handful stopped.

But that day I scored big! A stranger dropped a big, fat $20 bill into my palms. I felt rich. And guilty. This $20 bill made the next two days easier. It paid for hot McDonald's coffee and a few subway rides, which I used to get out of the March snow. My other meals were free, provided by volunteers at soup kitchens or mobile food carts.

The first night I reconvened with six friends for safety as dark settled in. We huddled under a pile of blankets in hopes of sleep on the sidewalk in front of the Martin Luther King, Jr. Public Library.

Around midnight, I peered out of a slit in the blankets as a volunteer pulled up, walked from their van, and spread extra blankets across the top of our pile. *Wow, someone would do that for an anonymous pile of homeless people?!*

Two hours later, I woke from a light sleep to a friend shouting and swatting our pile of blankets. He was swatting out a matchbook—*a matchbook*—that had been lit and dutifully tossed on our pile by a group of teens that snickered as they ran away. *Wow, someone would actually do that to an anonymous pile of homeless people?*

I didn't sleep well after that. Fear and anger haunted my vacant dreams.

The following night, a church opened its parish as emergency shelter from the even colder temperatures. That night, inside and warm, I was able to simply listen. As I chatted with my shelter mates, I heard stories I could have never fathomed. Businessmen who couldn't beat their drug addictions despite repeated attempts, war veterans who couldn't get out of the cycle of poverty.

Today, as I watch our market economy mercilessly toss these folks aside, I can't help but wonder which of them made it and which ones did not.

American Homeowner Preservation (AHP)

American Homeowner Preservation (AHP) buys distressed mortgages from banks to help families avoid foreclosure. Born during the Great Recession (thanks Wall Street) when 10 million families lost their homes to foreclosure, AHP works with families to keep them *in* their homes instead of kicking them out.

Now, anyone can invest with AHP in keeping families in their homes with as little as $100.

How to Keep People in Their Homes

Mortgage holders like banks often sell "non-performing" mortgages. This means the company that gave you a mortgage could sell it off to some other company. Since homeowners who can't pay their mortgage mean lost money to a typical bank, the banks will sell large groups of these mortgages to other companies who buy them at deep discounts, now own those houses, and sell off the houses (and kick the owners out) to make a nice little profit.

Instead of acting like every other bank, AHP buys the non-performing mortgages at deep discounts and shares those discounts with the people living in the homes. They work with homeowners to reduce payments and eliminate negative equity. AHP collects mortgage payments, keeps the owners in their homes, and has enough upside to pay everyday investors like us a return on their investment.

Why Homeownership

AHP believes homeownership improves lives. Research shows that:
- Homeowners vote and participate in communities more than non-homeowners.
- Children of homeowners perform higher on academic achievement tests, have fewer behavior problems, and are more likely to finish high school.[xii]

When you invest with AHP, you are actually purchasing equity ownership in their company—like owning a portion of a company through stock. As a shareholder, you get paid a dividend every month on the amount you invest. Your principal is paid back in five years.

If you had invested in the 2015 fund, you would have received a 12% return each year. The most recent fund targets a 10% return for investors.[33]

Term: 5 years[34]
Target Return: 10%
Minimum Investment: $100

Guerrilla Development

Guerrilla Development develops edgy in-fill buildings in Portland, OR with a goal of making neighborhoods more desirable. Their buildings are endowed with aptly Portland names like: *Ode to Rose's* and *Atomic Orchard Experiment*. The *Fair-Haired Dumbbell* is covered entirely by grafitti-esque paintings.

---

[33] As of 2019.
[34] AHP aims to pay back principal and interest in 5 years, but it could be shorter or longer

Homeless Transitions

Take heart, Guerrilla Development has a conscience. In a city where 4,000 people don't have permanent housing and 2,000 will sleep on the street tonight, Guerrilla is attempting to do its part. A new building, *Jolene's First Cousin*, will feature 11 single rooms to help house people transitioning out of homelessness. The building features a shared kitchen, living and dining room, and a courtyard. Street Roots, which provides jobs and resources for homeless people, helps place individuals. The monthly rent is $425 and is partly subsidized by the other market rate lofts and retail units in the development.

Portland's Got Their Back

For all the talk about affordable housing, or elected officials have done very little. So Guerrilla went to the people. In 2017, Guerrilla **raised funds**

from Oregon residents to help fund *Jolene's First Cousin.* **The investment offering sold out in 3 days and raised $300,000**[35]. They're planning on many more Jolene's-style developments in the future.

Guerrilla's first public offering was a note with a fixed return. To find out about future offerings, sign up for notifications from Guerrilla.

Example offering: Jolene's First Cousin[36]

Type: Fixed Return Term: 10 years Target Return: 5% Minimum investment: $3,000

Enterprise Community Partners

Enterprise Community Partners has helped build or renovate nearly 100,000 affordable homes. They help provide early-stage financing for projects like the Gateways Apartments in Los Angeles, where slow wage growth and a high cost of living pushed homelessness up 12% from 2013 to 2017. The apartments feature affordable housing with support services that have been shown to be one of the most sustainable solutions for shifting chronically homeless individuals out of homelessness. Gateways supports 70 full-time jobs, some filled by formerly homeless individuals. While typically thought of as a cost burden, Enterprise has shown that permanent supportive housing in Los Angeles generates annual health care savings of $19,000 per person.

---

[35] This offering was only open to residents of Oregon.

[36] Pro tip: For any wanna-be developers out there, Guerrilla hosts the Excel Pro forma financial spreadsheet for each project on their website.

Impact Snapshot:

Enterprise Community Partners has supported projects like:

- 500 affordable homes at CAMBA Gardens in Brooklyn, NY, built to one of the highest environmental building standards—LEED Platinum.
- Support for Bay Area Transit-Oriented Affordable Housing Fund, the development of affordable housing and other community services near transit lines in the San Francisco Bay Area.
- Providing funding to Chicago Southland Community Development Loan Fund, which develops areas within one half-mile of Metra or South Shore stations and high-frequency bus routes.

An investment in the Enterprise Community Loan Fund is a note with a fixed return.

Term & Interest Rate:
1 year, 0.85%
2 year, 1.5%
3 year, 2.0%
5 year, 2.5%
7 year, 3.0%
10 year, 3.5%

Minimum Investment: $5,000

Small Change

Small Change believes purpose-built real estate can significantly improve blighted neighborhoods and open opportunities to low-income communities.

Small Change's platform lets you search for and invest directly in real estate projects in the U.S. that meet Small Change's Change Index. For example, a revitalization project in Baltimore's Oliver neighborhood—best known for its role in HBO's "The Wire"—raised funds on Small Change in 2018. In 2019, Restore Neighborhoods L.A. crowdfunded an affordable housing project with a 9% target return for investors.

Not Just Real Estate: The Change Index

Small Change only accepts projects that meet Change Index criteria. Their Change Index measures:

- Mobility — 7 measurements like bike-ability, walkability, and public transport
- Community — 7 measurements like fresh food access and affordable housing
- Economic Vitality — 7 measurements like number of jobs created and diverse workforce

A few projects funded through Small Change:
- Pittsburgh, PA — Repositioning and renovating the historic six-story Liberty Bank Building into a cowork space and small business resource. The project raised $300,000 from 19 investors and aims to deliver a 10% return over 3 years.
- New Orleans, LA — The building of several beautiful starter homes in the inner-city. The project raised $95,000 from 39 investors with a 15-month term and an estimated return of 8%.
- Capitol Heights, MD / Washington DC — A renovation to increase the bedroom count of units in a 44-unit, affordable residential project. The project raised $200,000 from 13 investors with a target 10% return.

An investment with a Small Change project is an equity investment with a target return based on performance of the project.

Terms: 1-5 years
Interest: 6%-28%
Minimum Investment: $500

Affordable Homes of South Texas

Affordable Homes of South Texas (AHST) sells homes at cost with 0% mortgages to individuals and families earning under 80% of area median income.

Founded in 1976, AHST serves people like Mr. Mata, a single father of two children who lost his wife in an accident. Mr. Mata's credit wasn't good enough for banks and he didn't have the money for a down payment. AHST helped him find a quality home he could afford, so he could begin building equity and have a stable place to raise his kids.

AHST's loan portfolio is backed by $50 million in assets and 40+ years of experience.

An investment in AHST's Hope Fund is a note with a fixed return.

Term and Interest Rates: 1 year – 1.5% 3 year – 2.0% 5 year – 3.0% 7 year – 3.25% 10 year – 3.5% Minimum Investment: $100

Affordable Housing Non-profits

If you want to create impact close to home and the investments above don't serve your area, there are dozens of amazing non-profits and development companies that don't offer investment opportunities, but rely heavily on donations and community support:

- Eden Housing (California)
- Foundation Communities (Texas)
- AHC, Inc. (Virginia, Maryland Area)
- Aeon (Minneapolis)
- Chicanos Por la Causa (Southwest US)
- Community Development and Preservation Corporation (Washington D.C.)
- Hispanic Housing Development Corporation (Chicago)

- Homes for America (Mid-Atlantic states)
- LINC Housing (Southern California)
- Mercy Housing (38,000 homes in 41 states)
- Nevada HAND Inc. (Nevada and Las Vegas)
- NHP Foundation (6,000 homes in 16 states)
- Preservation of Affordable Housing (9,000 homes in 9 states)

Affordable Housing—Review

You can put your money to work with companies developing affordable housing and keeping homeowners in homes.

- The U.S. has a shortage of 7.4 million affordable rental homes available to extremely-low-income renter households.
- 21 million Americans spend more than 30% of their income to afford rent.
- It's harder than ever to afford a home for our middle class workforce and our most vulnerable income populations.

Investment	Min. Investment	Target Return	Term
American Homeowner Preservation (AHP)	$100	10%	5 years
Small Change	$500	6-10%	2 years
Enterprise Community Partners	$5,000	1%-3.5%	1-10 years
Guerrilla Development	$500	5%	5 years
Affordable Homes of South texas	$100	1.5%-3.25%	1-10 years

Renewable Energy

It's uncertain how 10 billion people will power their lives. But if we're looking for cheaper, more reliable, and cleaner energy, renewable energy is the answer.

Lazard's 2017 *Levelized Cost of Energy Analysis* highlighted that wind and solar energy are now cheaper than diesel, nuclear, coal and in most cases natural gas.[37] In 2019, Los Angeles Power & Water inked a deal to buy energy from a solar energy farm with battery storage—at half the cost of power from a new natural gas plant. According to the International Energy Agency, 41% of global energy spending was invested in renewables in 2017.

Cost and carbon reductions aside, renewables have the profound potential to bring electricity to the 1 billion people who still don't have access to it. In India and Africa, wind and solar can leap frog expensive transmission lines and the pollution and environmental devastation that come with coal power.

I can say for certain I'm grateful that the world we're building for our children grandchildren will breathe a little easier. As an investor, I put my money where my mouth—and lungs—are, with investments in several of the investments in this chapter.

Investments Ahead

YieldCos | Companies that own large renewable energy projects and pay out solid dividends to investors like us.

Renewable Energy ETFs | Collections of renewable energy stocks that allow you to invest in a diverse group of companies that benefit from renewable energy growth.

---

[37] Lazard's Levelized Cost Of Energy Analysis Version 11.0 Lazard isn't some left-leaning think tank. Founded in 1848, Lazard is a hard-charging investment bank operating in 27 countries. Their objective analysis proves that given time and investment, renewable energy is more efficient than old school sources.

Clean Energy Credit Union | A modern, democratically-owned bank that also makes loans to people putting solar panels on their homes.

Solar Bonds | Several fixed return investments that finance the installation of solar panels around the world.

Renewable Energy YieldCos

YieldCos own large renewable energy generation projects, like wind and solar farms, and are one of the best investments most people don't know about.

YieldCo comes from *Yield Company*, a special structure of company that pays a yield, or dividend, every three months to its investors. YieldCos own power generation facilities—like large solar farms and the wind farms you see on the side of the interstate—and sell the electricity they produce to power companies through long-term contracts.[38]

Here's an example: One of the top rated YieldCos is Pattern Energy Group (PEGI), which owns 25 wind and solar projects in the U.S. and internationally. Pattern Energy uses its cash flow from selling electricity to pay its shareholders $1.69 for every share they own. While writing, its share price was $18, meaning when you invest $18 you own a share and earn a 9.4% return just for owning the stock.[39] Because the stock is traded like any other stock, it could go up or down, too, meaning your $18 could also increase in value.

YieldCo Benefits

YieldCos are one of my favorite investments not only because they supply clean energy, they offer compelling financial benefits, too.

Easy to Buy and Sell | YieldCos trade on the stock market and you can buy them through any brokerage account, like Vanguard or TDAmeritrade.

---

[38] Note: Not all YieldCos own 100% renewable energy assets. Some of them own conventional energy producing facilities, or transmission lines and other infrastructure projects. I've tried to make notes where this is true, but please research each company before investing to make sure their projects suit your investment needs and values.

[39] Dividend and share price at time of writing. Share price fluctuates daily and dividends may be changed every three months.

Strong Dividends | In 2015, the average dividend yield of listed YieldCos was 6.2%, with a range of 3%-15%.

Lower Risk | YieldCos generally own a diverse mix of mature energy generation facilities that have long-term contracts that ensure large power companies buy energy from them. Company maturity, plus long term contracts equals more stability[40].

Tax Efficiency | The dividend earnings from owning a YieldCo are generally classified as dividends (Form 1099 on your taxes), which are taxed at a lower rate than income.[41]

Transparency | Most YieldCos list the locations and types of their power generation facilities. This is a great way to know exactly what you own.

Adrian's Aside: YieldCo Nerd Timeout

I assume my fellow corporate-structure-and-renewable-energy nerds are curious about how these things work.

YieldCos are side companies started by larger parent companies like your local energy utility or Brookfield Asset Management, a global asset manager with $285 billion in assets under management. The parent company owns a majority of the YieldCo and sells the rest to investors like us. By using this structure, these companies get certain legal tax benefits and can raise money to help finance new energy installations. Each share we own is a small piece of the company, just like a traditional share of stock.

YieldCos came on the scene in the early 2010s and boomed from 2013 to mid-2015, when the ballooning YieldCo bubble burst. Much like the Dotcom bubble, investors bid up YieldCo share prices without anything to back up the growth. Luckily, the bubble popped without much carnage and the market has returned to what one analyst calls "nearing normalcy."

---

[40] This does not mean *no* risk. YieldCos can fluctuate just like Google or Snapchat.

[41] I am not a tax advisor, nor do I play one on TV. Please consult a tax advisor, as I am in no way offering tax advice.

Top 8 YieldCos

There are about 20 publicly traded YieldCos. Here's a look at those considered the Top 8.

*****A typical house roof might have 5kW of solar energy, so every 3,000 megawatts listed below can be thought of like roughly 600,000 rooftops of solar panels.*

YieldCo Company Name and Stock Ticker	Dividend Yield Target	Megawatts of renewable energy	Locations of projects
NextEra Energy (NEP)	3.6%	2,926	N. America
TerraForm Power (TERP)	6.51%	2,606	US, Canada, UK, Chile, Portugal, Spain, Uruguay
Pattern Energy Group (PEGI)	9.00%	2,644	US, Canada, Chile
TransAlta Renewables (TRSWF)	8.06%	2,441[42]	Canada, Wyoming, Australia
Atlantica Yield (AY)	6.65%	1,446	N. America, S. America
Clearway Energy Inc. (CWEN.A)	6.15%	3,170[43]	US
Hannon Armstrong Sustainable Infrastructure (HASI)	6.11%[44]	5,000[45]	US
Brookfield Renewable Partners (BEP)	5.3%	17,400[46]	N. America, S. America, Europe, Asia

[42] This includes 13 hydroelectric facilities, 8 natural gas facilities, and 1 natural gas pipeline.
[43] This company also owns other assets including conventional fossil fuel energy facilities.
[44] Hannon Armstrong qualifies as a Real Estate Investment Trust, which may impact your taxation.
[45] Hannon Armstrong also focuses on energy efficiency and water reduction projects.
[46] Primarily hydropower, with some solar, wind, and energy storage.

Own Multiple YieldCos

If you want to diversify your investments across multiple YieldCos without investing in each one independently (which incurs a new fee for each transaction with a typical brokerage) there is **GlobalX YieldCo ETF (YLCO),** an exchange-traded fund (ETF) that holds many of the top YieldCos. Because the yield is averaged across the holdings, it yields 4.1%. The expense ratio, or fees, are 0.66%, which is a little higher than preferred (under 0.50% is preferred).

ETFs for Renewable Energy

ETFs are exchange-traded funds that allow you to invest in broad collection of publicly traded companies (ETFs, Index funds, and Mutual funds discussed fully in A More Sustainable Stock Market chapter. Here are two ETFs that can help you invest in the growth of clean, renewable energy.

Invesco Solar ETF (TAN) | This ETF invests in 23 companies in the solar industry, ranging from solar panel manufacturers to utilities to financiers. The expense ratio is a bit high at 0.74% and the ETF price is fairly volatile, but if you're betting on the future of the solar power industry, this ETF might be a good bet for you.

iShares Global Clean Energy ETF (ICLN) | This ETF invests in 30 companies that are global leaders in solar power, waste-to-energy, and geothermal. The expense ratio is a more reasonable 0.47%.

Clean Energy Credit Union

Clean Energy Credit Union is a modern bank—technically a credit union—that gives its customers votes and uses the money saved with it to finance renewable energy projects, like solar panels, clean energy vehicles, and green home improvements.

For more details, see Clean Energy Credit Union in the Banking for Good chapter.

Solar Bonds

If you want to earn a fixed return while investing in renewable energy, there are a handful of companies that offer solar bonds.

Wunder Capital[47]

In 2017, Wunder Capital financed 115 solar projects on business rooftops for a total of 37 Megawatts of solar—the equivalent of about 7,400 rooftops worth of solar or 818 semi trucks filled with coal.[48] A few of these projects include a solar farm for the California Department of Water & Power, a 435 kilowatt solar system for a Washington DC public charter school, and a 1,000 kW system for an Ohio school district.

Wunder Capital's two funds (open to accredited investors) deliver impressive returns from 6 to 7.5% while taking huge strides for renewable energy.

According to Wunder, an offering for non-accredited investors is in the works.

Wunder Income Fund

Target Return: 6%
Term: 10 years
Minimum Investment: $1,000

Wunder Capital 5

Target Return: 7.5%
Term: 5 years
Minimum Investment: $1,000

---

[47] Open to Accredited Investors. An offering for non-accredited investors is in the works.
[48] About 36 million pounds of coal.

Solar City Solar Bonds

Solar City, now owned by Tesla, is the U.S.'s largest solar employer with over 285,000 customers. Solar City has previously offered attractive solar bonds for everyday investors with returns from 4% to 6.5%, but they didn't have any offerings open at the time of writing.

> Return: 4%-6.5%
> Terms: 1-5 years
> Minimum Investment: $1,000

CoPower

CoPower allows Canadian residents to invest in large-scale solar installations, energy efficiency improvements, LED lighting upgrades, and geothermal heating & cooling.

> Target Return: 5%
> Term: 6 year
> Minimum Investment: $5,000

SunPower

Designed for high-rollers, SunFunder is an investment for accredited investors who want to help bring solar to off-grid places around the world.

SunFunder lends to leading solar companies in Uganda, Tanzania, and India, with current investors like the Rockefeller Foundation and Leonardo DiCaprio Foundation.

> Target Return: 5%*
> Term: 2-3 years
> Minimum Investment: $250,000

*SunFunder charges a 3% management fee for assets under management.

Abundance Investments

Abundance Investments, the U.K.'s first crowdfunding platform, has already invested over £75 million in renewable energy projects and affordable housing. Tell your friends across the pond.

Term: 3-16 years
Return: 4%-12%
Minimum Investment: £5

Renewable Energy—Review

Renewable energy for the win! As our planet makes it way toward 10 billion people, energy that is cheaper, cleaner, and more reliable can help us breath easier. These investments generate impressive returns, too.

- Wind and solar energy have become cheaper than coal and nuclear.
- The future is bright for solar. In 2019, Los Angeles Power & Water inked a deal to buy energy from solar energy farm with battery storage—at half the cost of power from a new natural gas plant.
- A $15,000 investment could save 10,000 pounds of coal burned for electricity.
- YieldCos are one of the best investments people don't know about—offering attractive returns from clean energy projects.
- Use your savings account to finance solar projects with Clean Energy Credit Union.

Investment	Min. Investment	Target Return	Term
YieldCos	$20	3-9+%	None
Renewable Energy ETFs	$50	2-20%	None
Clean Energy Credit Union CD	$1,000	1.55%	5-10 years
Solar City Solar Bonds	$1,000	4-6.5%	1-5 years
Wunder Capital Income Fund	$1,000	6%	10 years
Wunder Capital 5	$1,000	7.50%	5 years
SunFunder	$250,000	5%	2 years
CoPower Canada	$5,000	5%	5 years
Abundance Investments UK	$5	4%-12%	3-16 years

Banking for Good

One common theme emerges when talking with changemakers: They take action where they are most passionate. The handy ones install solar panels on their rental homes. Others donate blood. Some turn their homes into *zero waste* households while others write books to share wisdom. We always do our best.

But who's passionate about where they bank? So our savings accounts are left with the bank with the most branches near us, or the one are parents used.

Banking matters. Why? Because banks take the billions of dollars we give them to hold on to for safe keeping and *they choose* what to finance with it. Odds are your bank loaned money to finance the Dakota Access Pipeline and you didn't know about it. Even if you did, there's little you could do.

I wanted to test my *little-ol-me-power*, so in 2016 I wrote a letter to Wells Fargo. I shared—kindly, of course—I preferred my money not be a part of the $120 million they loaned to the Dakota Access Pipeline. I wasn't the only one. Thousands of customers wrote their banks. **Seattle's City Council even voted to stop doing business with Wells Fargo.**

Wells Fargo wrote me back. It turns out enough *little-ol-me's* sent enough letters to at least get their attention. The response: "We've enhanced our own due diligence in sectors subject to our Environmental and Social Risk Management policy."

Wrong answer, Wells Fargo. It became clear that poor leadership and lack of ethical company culture isn't confined to one decision when Wells Fargo was found to have created millions of fraudulent savings and checking accounts on behalf of customers without their consent. They then charged these people fees and sent them debit cards they didn't ask for. Thankfully, thousands of customers have left the bank and they were fined $185 million. Additional civil suits may cost the bank $2.8 billion.

Now what if you could bank with a company whose values matched your own? The rise in conscious consumers has been met by a rise in conscious banks. In this chapter, we'll look at banking options where impact is only a few clicks away.

Investments Ahead

Local Banking | Local banks typically loan a certain percentage of their funds in your own community, with small businesses you frequent. Learn how to find a bank or credit union near you.

Amalgamated Bank | The largest union-owned bank in the U.S. and the first to raise employee minimum wages to $15 per hour. Amalgamated is the leading bank for do-gooders.

Clean Energy Credit Union | A democratically run bank that uses its assets to fund renewable energy projects. The bank is online and accessible from everywhere.

Aspiration's Spend & Save | The online financial firm has high-interest checking and savings accounts that also rates the companies where people spend their money through its Aspiration Impact Measurement of people and planet.

Good Money | A brand new online bank that is owned by its customers and doles out 50% of profits to fund sustainable initiatives.

Local Banking

Banking locally is one of the easiest ways to make a difference in your community. Community banks and credit unions prefer to make loans to local businesses and families, not hedge funds. This money stays in your community, supports places you actually use, and has greater oversight.

Search "Green America Break Up With Your Mega Bank" (or go to www.adrianreif.com/dogoodersguide to find the link) to find a national database of local banks and credit unions.

Amalgamated Bank

Amalgamated Bank is a bank with longstanding values. I try to contain my opinion in this book, but after three years of research and becoming a customer, I can't help but send sincere appreciation to a bank like Amalgamated.

Founded in 1923 by the Amalgamated Clothing Workers of America, Amalgamated is now the largest union-owned bank in the U.S. They are a Certified B Corp, a member of the Global Alliance for Banking on Values, and powered by 100% renewable energy.

In 2015, they became the first bank to raise all employee wages to a minimum of $15 per hour. Their CEO-to-worker pay ratio is 17:1, far more equitable than most large banks. In 2016, Amalgamated launched another first, a service that gave home buyers downpayment protection in case the market changes quickly.

The company offers free online banking for individuals and businesses with competitive interest rates. The Give Back savings account pays out 1% interest that is matched 50% by Amalgamated and is donated to a non-profit of your choice.

Savings Interest Rate: 1% - 1.65%
Term: Unlimited
Minimum Investment: $1

Clean Energy Credit Union

Clean Energy Credit Union is a democratically run bank that uses its assets to lend money to renewable energy projects, like solar panels, clean energy vehicles, and green home improvements.

Its initiator, Blake Jones, also co-founded Namaste Solar, which has installed over 5,000 solar energy systems since 2004. Blake took the challenge he faced at Namaste—it was hard for people interested in installing solar panels to find upfront financing—and with the Clean Energy team set out to solve this problem.

Impact Snapshot:

- A $15,000 deposit could be loaned out to finance a 6 kilowatt solar panel system, preventing over 12,000 tons of carbon emissions per year (for 30+ years).
- The bank is online, which keeps costs down.
- CECU is a credit union, which are democratically-owned and controlled by their members on a one-member-one-vote basis.

Savings Account*

Target Return: Modest interest rate, goes up with higher balances Term: Unlimited Minimum Investment: $5

Clean Energy CD

Target Return: 1.5% (goes up based on amount and term) Term: 5-year, 10-year Minimum Investment: $1,000

*Like all online banks, you can easily transfer funds between your accounts at Clean Energy Credit Union and other financial institutions via free ACH transfers.

Aspiration Spend & Save

Aspiration is an investment firm that emerged to help do-gooders like you invest with simplicity. The company mirrors the values of a new generation: high-performance, transparency, and idealism.[49] Aspiration's CEO, Andrei Cherny, built the bank for everyday people—who have the deck stacked against them when it comes to finances—after a long career spanning the White House, the Consumer Financial Protection Bureau, and as a financial fraud prosecutor.

---

[49] More about the company in A More Sustainable Stock Market and Online Platforms chapters.

The online bank features a checking account—Spend—and a savings account—Save.[50] These accounts feature interest rates far above the national average (if you set up a recurring deposit) and no fees.

Aspiration set a new bar when they launched the Aspiration Impact Measurement (AIM) in 2018, which scores the companies you spend money at and rates them on equity and sustainability. They published their "Nice List" just before Black Friday, sharing the Top 10 companies on social and environmental values, following through on their mission to help do-gooders use their money wisely.

To round it out, if you invest with Aspiration you can "pay what is fair" by sliding a scale from 0% to 2%. And Aspiration donates a dime of every dollar they earn to expand economic opportunity for struggling Americans.

Target Return: 2%
Term: Endless
Minimum Investment: $100

Good Money

Good Money is a revolutionary when it comes to banking. They are on a mission to "cancel the endless cycles of extractive capitalism." This online bank is owned by its customers, whose share values increase as the bank grows. It invests or donates 50% of its profits in social and environmental organizations.

Good Money was giving out ownership to customers who joined the waitlist at the time of writing.

Target Return: 2%-50%[51]
Term: Endless
Minimum Investment: $100

[50] Nailed the simplicity!
[51] Good Money estimates the shares you receive for joining will be worth a lot more in the decades to come.

Banking for Good—Review

Take the easy step of switching to a bank that matches your values. It costs nothing—except a little time—but the benefits may be worth it.

- U.S. banks hold $16 trillion in assets and lend that money out to finance things you may not support.
- Local banks and credit unions often circulate money in their communities, supporting the businesses and neighbors you know.
- Amalgamated, a 96-year-old bank is union-owned, pays it workers fair wages, and is powered by renewable energy.
- A new breed of banks—like Clean Energy Credit Union, Aspiration, and Good Money—fund sustainable projects with your money and listen to their customers. You could even potentially be an owner.

Organization	Impact Areas	Services
Local Banking	Money often stays in your community	Search "Green America Break Up With Your Mega Bank"
Amalgamated Bank	Union-owned, pays workers well, 17:1 CEO to worker pay ratio, 100% renewable energy powered	Convenient online banking
Clean Energy Credit Union	Lends money for solar panels	Convenient online banking
Aspiration	Expand financial access for everyone; Donates 10% to microloans for struggling Americans.	Convenient online banking; Low-fee mutual funds
Good Money	Customer-owned; 50% of profits to global impact	Convenient online banking

Food System

The *Food System* is an inextricable and intricately linked network of epic proportions.

To get the 730,000 calories that each of us chow down per year, we must rely on tiny microbes in the soil.[52] And pollinators like birds and bees, which pollinate somewhere between 78% to 95% of flowering plants.[53] And the 525 *million* farms around the world.[xiii]

For much of my life, I was blissfully unaware of this ineffably important web. My knowledge of farming was solely dependent on my father's stories of growing up on a Wisconsin farm, where he recalls milking dozens of cows as the sun rose, throwing hay bales onto trailers for days at a time, and dinners made mostly from food grown on the farm. I can almost smell my grandmother's food cellar, the shelves filled with gurgling crocks of fermenting cabbage and canned goods.

Many years ago, I moved back to my Wisconsin homeland and began selling food at a handful of farmers markets. Despite earning the Gardening merit badge in Boy Scouts, I knew little about the food web. I spent countless hours next to farmers, their tables piled high with kale, tomatoes, honey, and squash.

The more I asked, the more I began to understand. I learned how to cook parsnips and rutabaga and pre-ordered Thanksgiving turkey from a community farm. One summer, I even volunteered on a CSA farm in exchange for a hefty box of fresh food.

While I'm no expert on the food system, it's become abundantly clear that we must ensure the health of our soil and our farmers if we want to achieve a happy, healthy planet.

Currently, we face a noble challenge. Lands are overgrazed, undernourished.

---

[52] There are between 100 million and one billion bacteria in an average gram of soil

[53] Estimates of flowering plants that require pollination by animals are between 78% in temperate regions and 94% in tropical regions (Ollerton et al. 2011, Oikos 120:321-326).

Fisheries are collapsing. Phosphorus runs from heavily-sprayed fields into streams and lakes, choking these precious waters.

The answers are simple: support soil health and support the farmers who champion it. The Regenerative Agriculture movement is gaining steam, as it helps farmers increase yields and profitability while increasing biodiversity, improving soil health, and capturing carbon in the soil.

In this chapter, you'll see several investable efforts that are a part of the movement to reimagine our food system and restore the health of our land.

**While there are some great investments to help support a healthy food system, simple acts are just as powerful. Spend money at the farmer's market, buy from responsible and transparent companies like Alter-Eco, Equal Exchange, Organic Valley, and Patagonia Provisions, which source from small and organic farmers around the world. If you want to up your game, search for "Regenerative Agriculture" and read up on it. I have a list of top articles selected at adrianreif.com/dogoodersguide if you want a head start. In short, vote with your calories!

Investments Ahead

RSF Social Finance | RSF's collaborative loan funds support entrepreneurs solving food system challenges, including a fund directed to women-led businesses.

Organic Valley | The largest farmer-owned supplier of organic milk in the U.S. offers an investment in their company from time to time.

Local Investing | Use the platforms listed to find innovative, local food companies raising money.

Iroquois Valley Farms | An innovative company financing farmland transition to organic and regenerative farming.

RSF Social Finance

RSF Social Finance is an innovative non-profit that supports entrepreneurs working to solve complex social and environmental problems in our food system.

> **"We envision a world in which money serves the highest intentions of the human spirit and contributes to an economy based on generosity and interconnectedness."**
> **-RSF Vision**

RSF is imbued by the spirit of its founder, Austrian philosopher and scientist Rudolf Steiner. **Steiner understood money to be a bridge that connects human beings and serves economic initiatives.** He "encouraged the world to strive for a less hierarchical, more networked mutual approach to business leadership—one that realizes the potential of economic collaboration."

Impact Snapshot:

Since 1984, RSF has been working hard to transition money to achieve their vision and empower food system entrepreneurs.

- $450 million directed to transformational entrepreneurs.
- Created a network of 1,600 conscious investors.
- Pioneered collaborative investment approach where RSF's investors and borrowers decide on loan interest rates together.
- 100% repayment to investors since 1984

Portfolio Examples

Here are a few examples of who RSF lends to:

- **Veritable Vegetable** | A woman-owned organic produce distributor.

- **Hana Health** | Improves health and wellness in the remote region of Hana, Maui among Native Hawaiians and other underserved populations.
- **RecycleForce** | Offers much-needed electronics recycling while training former inmates with job skills.
- **Crown O'Maine Organic Cooperative** | Leading distributor of local organic produce in Maine.
- **DC Central Kitchen** | Job skills for at-risk adults and balanced meals for shelters and low-income schools.
- **Fibershed** | Develops regenerative textile systems. Think small-scale wool farmers.
- **Guayaki** | Importer of yerba mate with a mission to restore 200,000 acres of rainforest and provide 1,000 living wage jobs in South America.

Women's Collaborative

In 2018, RSF's Women's Capital Collaborative (WCC) distributed $1 million in loans to women-led enterprises around the world.

"The WCC addresses a market failure for women, who have a more difficult time fundraising and face many more barriers than men," says an RSF senior director.

An investment with RSF is a note with a fixed return.

RSF Social Investment Fund Note

Target Return: 1%
Term: 90-day term; renew or redeem
Minimum investment: $1,000

RSF Food System Transformation Fund & Regenerative Economy Fund

Target Return: 1%
Term: 5 years
Minimum investment: $100,000

*These funds provide even bigger loans focused on food system improvement.

Organic Valley

Organic Valley is the largest supplier of organic milk in the U.S., the largest organic *farmer-owned* cooperative in the world, and one of the few privately-owned companies you can invest in. They ensure a fair price is paid to their farmers.

Organic Valley is a cooperative company, meaning they source their milk and beef from **over 1,800 farmers in 36 states who are also owners of the company.** Each farmer-owner has a voice in determining growth, profit sharing, best practices, and other cooperative fundamentals.

You'll see Organic Valley's cows and farmers on the front of gallons of milk, blocks of cheese, and pasture-fed beef in almost every grocery store in the U.S. and many markets abroad.

Organic Valley formed in a rural Wisconsin farming community in 1988 and is still headquartered there. They now have sales over $1 billion as they've become one of the highest quality and most efficient producers of organic dairy in the world. *Turns out supporting your farmers is a good business strategy, too.*

Because the co-op is not beholden to shareholders or outside investors, the business can prioritize paying farmers a stable price each month, as well as providing other valuable shared services, such as world-class veterinary care, and soil and pasture improvement programs.

From time to time, Organic Valley offers "preferred stock"[54] for sale to the public. The preferred stock offers a 4% dividend, meaning they pay you 4% interest on the amount you've invested. At the time of writing, Organic Valley was offering a Class E, Series 4 preferred stock with the following terms:

---

[54] Preferred-stock is simply a class of stock with certain rights and benefits. When you buy a stock market stock, you are usually buying a non-preferred or common stock. Organic Valley's preferred stock offers a dividend payment, but is non-voting, which means you can't vote in company affairs. The farmer-owners' shares of stock do allow them to vote in company affairs.

Class E, Series 4[55]

Return: 4%
Term: Until sold back to the company
Minimum Investment: $5,000

Direct Investments in Local Food Companies

While large, system-focused investments may be hard to find, you can invest in food system change by finding local companies in your community or state.

For example, California residents invested in a local butcher shop in Berkeley and Massachusetts residents invested in the Dorchester Community Co-op, both companies offering better-for-you and better-for-the-planet business models.

Several platforms can help you local food companies, farmers, and more:

- Investibule.co (search "Food & Bev" or "Co-op")
- CuttingEdgeX
- Slow Money

These investments can range from low-interest loans to equity investments with high-potential payoffs. See the Local Investing and Crowdfunding chapters to learn more about each platform.

Iroquois Valley Farms

Iroquois Valley Farms is an innovative farm and finance company that focuses on healthy ecosystems while helping to put organic farmers on land. They are featured in the Nature Investing chapter.

---

[55] To cover my legal bases, you should rely only on the information contained in Organic Valley's Offering Circular.

Food System—Review

The food system is a vast web that supports all life on our planet.

- Epic land degradation, the collapse of ocean fisheries, and food inequality can all be transformed through investment in our food system.
- RSF Social Finance supports transformative food system entrepreneurs.
- Organic Valley is owned by its organic farmers.
- Keep spending at your farmers' markets and vote with your calories.

Investment	Min. Investment	Target Return	Term
RSF Social Investment Fund Note	$1,000	1%	90 days
RSF Food System Transformation Fund	$100,000	1%	5 years
Organic Valley Preferred Stock	$5,000	4%	Until sold back to company
Direct Investments in Local Food Companies	$25	2%-50%[1]	1 -10 years

[1] The high end of this range is represented by an equity investment in a high-growth food company that is able to sell the company for a substantial profit. This would be a rare occurrence.

Investing In Nature

In a short thirty years, our planet could be carrying 10 billion people. We have an opportunity to ensure the health of nature so that all of us can access the resources we need to live happy, healthy lives. But it's going to take big investments in conserving nature. As Wendell Barry once wrote:

"What we do to the land, we do to ourselves."

Paying Mama Earth

To start, we've only recently begun to realize how critical nature is to our survival. Yes, we get our food from her, but just about everything else is supplied by nature, too. Scientists are beginning to help us wrap our heads around the importance of nature and the Ecosystem Services it provides, but are rarely paid for.

A team of scientists estimated **the value of biodiversity in all of the Americas as $24.3 trillion**, about the same as the United States gross domestic product.[xiv] The same report by the UN estimated that Asia could run out of fish within 30 years.

But pricing and conserving Mama Earth could be just how we keep her alive. Thanks to a study with the super-sexy title *"Global estimates of the value of ecosystems and their services in monetary units,"* we're beginning to understand just how valuable ecosystems are. The study analyzed 300 case studies across 10 different biomes to help **scientists assign dollar values to ecosystems based on what they provide to society.**

For example, one acre of temperate forest provides $1,255 of value (median) to society every year. Inland wetlands provide $10,700 per acre. And coral reefs provide a median value of $147,000 per acre. These datum are just what we can measure. Here is a list of the 22 services that nature provides for us.

Provisioning services
- Food
- Water
- Raw Materials
- Genetic resources
- Medicinal resources
- Ornamental resources

Regulating Services
- Air quality regulation
- Climate regulation
- Disturbance moderation
- Regulation of water flows
- Waste treatment
- Erosion prevention
- Nutrient cycling
- Pollination
- Biological control

Habitat services
- Nursery services
- Genetic diversity

Cultural services
- Esthetic information
- Recreation
- Inspiration
- Spiritual experience
- Cognitive development

The Human Footprint

If we divided the Earth's land surface evenly and gave it evenly to 9 billion people, each of us would get 4 acres—or 3 football fields—to use. *If you get scared easily, you may want to close your eyes now.*

The average person around the globe uses 5.6 acres per year. The average American uses 21 acres—19 football fields. By the way, a Bangladeshi uses 1 acre...and growing.

You may have already done the math, but I just typed this into my TI-83 graphing calculator and the result was: "WHOA NOT GOOD!" I hate to be tongue-in-cheek about the future of the planet, but its important we take this seriously.

Today humanity uses the equivalent of 1.7 Earths to provide the resources we use and absorb our waste.[56] This is called our Ecological Footprint. This means it takes Earth's ecosystems 1 year and 6 months to regenerate what we use in 1 year. As an analogue, imagine asking your accountant how long she recommends you spend 1.5 times your yearly salary.

As mentioned earlier, I'm not interested in being a Doomsday prophet. Too many already. But smarter people than me are suggesting we shape it up. World-renowned astrophysicist Stephen Hawking—whose calculator was probably way better calculator than my TI-83—suggested in the time leading up to his passing that we'd need to leave the planet within the next 100 years if our species is to survive.

But I don't want to leave this planet. I love it. I love its miraculousness. I love its graciousness and generosity. I believe we can create a planet that's balanced—ecosystems that thrive and support people who are thriving. It's doable and it will take a deep appreciation for—and some serious investment in—nature. Let's think ahead and prepare for a bright future. As the Great Law of Peace by the Iroquois Nation says:

"In every deliberation one must consider the impact on the seventh generation."

Let's take a look at investable opportunities that help preserve our strained planet.

Investments Ahead

Iroquois Valley Farms | This finance company invests in bringing more organic and regenerative farmland online and getting young farmers on it.

---

[56] Global Footprint Network

NatureVest | The Nature Conservancy's investment fund that helps critical ecosystems while creating economic benefit.

Tree Latte | A membership platform that makes it easy for everyone to plant trees, with a mission to plant 1 billion trees to help cool the planet, provide income for people around the world, boost soil health, and soak up CO2.

Iroquois Valley Farms

Iroquois Valley Farms is a *restorative farmland finance company*.[57] They use a unique investment model to transition more farmland into organic and regenerative farming production, while helping millennial farmers gain access to increasingly expensive farmland.

Transitioning farmland to organic and restorative production is critical for our future focuses because the approaches champion soil health, biodiversity, and carbon sequestration, all of which will make it possible to grow enough food for 10 billion people without outstripping nature.

Solving Big Problems

Iroquois Valley Farms' unique model addresses several big problems with win-win approaches.

Access to organic farmland

Problem	Farmland is increasingly expensive, making it harder for organic farmers to find land and earn a living.
Solution	Iroquois Valley Farms provides long term leases and mortgage financing instead of typical 1-3 year land lease arrangements, helping organic farmers get or stay on their farms.

---

[57] Say that five times fast!

Restorative investments

Problem	Most land or real estate investments rely on extractive economics. Impact investors have few options to invest in land, and specifically farmland.
Solution	Iroquois Valley Farms owns a pool of farmland investments that focus on restorative farming, which restores soil health, water quality, and pollinator populations. Now, impact investors can invest in land while preserving land.

Organic Food Supply

Problem	Only 1% of farmland in the U.S. is organic. But demand for organic food is outpacing organic production.
Solution	Investments directly subsidize farmland transition to organic status, which can be a long and costly process (3 years+ before organic certification).

The Next Generation of Farming

Iroquois Valley Farms **helps millennial farmers find and secure access to increasingly expensive land** through their Young Farmer Land Access Program. As a result, they are building a pipeline of future farmers who will become stewards of the land, water, and food supply.

Impact Snapshot

- 8,000+ acres under lease or mortgage.
- $50 million in farmland assets (with a focus on organic and regenerative farming).
- 72% of the company's farmers are millennial.

Iroquois Valley Farms' Mission

The company blends their unique financing model with a bold vision— something we hope to see more of.

- Enable the next generation of young farmers.

- Farm with healthy, humane and organic practices without GMOs, toxic pesticides, herbicides, fungicides, synthetic fertilizers or other harmful chemicals.
- Keep the farmers on the land by indefinitely renewing their leases and preferentially selling to the farm tenant.
- Grow a broad-based membership, reaching thousands of like-minded investors concerned about the health of people, the planet, and financial stability.
- Transition traditional investment capital from conventional trading and extractive practices to renewable and regenerative uses.
- Maintain a fairly valued, democratically governed enterprise enabling both members and farmers to enjoy a stable and profitable return on their farming investment.
- Protect farmland.

There are two ways to invest in Iroquois Valley Farms:

Soil Restoration Note—This note allows you to invest directly in the transition of conventional farmland to organic farmland. This note has 10 years of history.

The investment is a note with a fixed return. It is available for accredited investors only.*

Return – 2.5%
Term – 5 years, redeemable after first year
Minimum Investment – $25,000

Non-accredited Offerings — Iroquois Valley Farms plans to have an investment option for non-accredited, everyday investors opening in 2019, which will have lower investment minimums. Visit the "Invest" tab on their site to check in.

REIT Equity Shares — The first organic family farmer REIT in the U.S. REIT stands for Real Estate Investment Trust and is an investment structure that typically allows you to buy ownership in a diverse group of buildings or properties while earning a dividend. Instead of buildings, this

REIT is comprised of the company's ownership of organic farmland leases and mortgages.

The farmland REIT pays you a dividend-like return based on its performance and your ownership shares may fluctuate in value, with the potential to increase. Given land scarcity and value, the REIT's share prices have consistently grown in value over the last decade.

Target Return – 2-3%
Term – At least 7 years
Minimum Investment – $31,000

NatureVest

NatureVest is an investment in nature conservation launched by The Nature Conservancy (TNC), a non-profit founded in 1951. They manage the largest system of private nature reserves in the world. They've protected over 119 million acres of land, thousands of miles of rivers, and have over 100 marine conservation sites around the world.

To expand conservation, TNC needs to unlock more capital. NatureVest's goal is investing $1 billion in agriculture, fisheries, water, and land to help protect and restore important ecosystems.

Investment Examples

To date $12 million raised and invested in NatureVest. They've used the capital to finance innovative projects like:

- Reducing stormwater and pollution run-off into Chesapeake Bay, the U.S.'s most productive estuary.
- Expanding wildlife habitat by stitching together important migratory corridors in the Cascade Mountain Range of Washington and in the Blackfoot River Valley in Montana.
- Smoothing out livestock markets to reduce overgrazing in Kenya's ever-important grasslands.

An investment in NatureVest's Conservation Note is a note with a fixed return.

Terms and Return: 1 year, 0%-0.8% 3-years, 0%-1.4% 5-years, 0%-2.0% Minimum Investment: $25,000

Tree Latte

Tree Latte is on a mission to plant 1 billion trees in the next 10 years by making it uber simple for the everyday person to regularly plant trees.

Tree Latte is a premier membership platform that automatically plants trees every month for its members. A free membership plants one tree every month, while other "tree ballers," as they are called, can choose to plant 4 trees every month for $4, 7 trees for $8, and up.

While Tree Latte does not provide a financial return, members build up quite the carbon-sequestering portfolio. For example, planting 8 trees per month will sequester about 9,600 pounds of CO_2 every year. Translation: That offsets 5,000 pounds of coal from being burned every year.

Tree Latte will also offer a public crowdfunding option, where members can invest. See the recommendations in the Crowdfunding and Angel Investing chapter to learn how to invest like world-class angel investor.

Nature Investing—Review

10. Billion. People. And all of them rely on nature to survive. We have an opportunity to find balance with nature while sustaining ourselves.

- The current Ecological Footprint for humanity is 1.7X Earth's yearly resources.
- The expanding population and extractive economy are putting a strain never seen before on many ecosystems.
- We can move into balance with nature if we value the Ecosystems Services—like water purification, food production, pollination and more—that are the basis for our human economy.
- Inland wetlands can provide over $10,000 per acre per year in value to our economy. Some coral reefs account for over $100,000 per acre per year.
- Investments in preserving ecosystem health like rivers in Australia and organic farmland in the U.S. can generate positive financial returns.

Investment	Min. Investment	Target Return	Term
NatureVest Conservation Note	$25,000	0.8-2.0%	1-5 years
Iroquois Valley Farms Soil Restoration Note*	$25,000	2.50%	5 years
Iroquois Valley Farms REIT Equity Shares*	$31,000	2-3%	7 years
Iroquois Valley Farms Soil Restoration Note (Non-Accredited)**	$25,000	1.50%	1-3 years

*Accredited only **Anticipated 2019

A More Sustainable
Stock Market

For most everyday investors, the stock market is an important vehicle for investing and growing money. Several trillion has shifted into socially responsible stock market investments over the last decade and more is coming.

As I mentioned at the beginning of the book, companies that score high on sustainability measures have been outpacing lagging companies on financial performance and stock price growth. This is a good thing for do-gooders—and for the future of our planet.

The U.S. stock market is worth somewhere near $30 trillion. That doesn't include the bond market or international stocks. Several of the world's largest and highest performing companies are committed to using 100% renewable energy, in large part because their shareholders have asked them to. Companies like Google, Apple, New Balance, Virgin Media, ABInBev, BMW[58] are transitioning to 100% renewables to outpace their competitors, lock in cheap prices, and fulfill their responsibility to carbon reduction.

Companies are also reducing water usage, working towards zero-waste, increasing diversity and inclusion, and more, in an effort to evolve with a quickly shrinking planet.

Sustainability Pays

As you plan for your future, investing in a more sustainable stock market can help you grow your money.

Deutsche-Bank[59] analyzed 2,000 empirical studies from 1970s to now. Ninety-percent of the studies showed that sustainably focused investing

---

[58] To see the full list of 191 companies, go to www.there100.org.
[59] The world's 16th largest bank.

provided higher returns than passive investing.

The Vanguard FTSE Social Index (VFTSX) is an example of one fund that invests in companies that score higher than their peers on environmental, social, and corporate governance (ESG) factors. From January 2008 to October 2018, it grew 117%, outperforming its benchmark, the Russell 1000, which grew 107%. The S&P 500 grew 99%.

Sustainability Makes a Difference

But can choosing which companies you invest in actually make a difference?

The price of a stock is actually driven by simple supply versus demand. If more people decide to buy Apple's stock than people who want to sell it, the price will increase.[60] If everyone starts selling Apple's stock, there's more supply of it than demand and the price drops.

Investing in a company's stock provides both tangible and intangible support for the company. If the stock price is strong, the company's balance sheet allows it to do more stuff, like invest in equipment, grow, pay dividends to investors, etc. This is tangible support. Your ownership also sends an intangible signal that you expect the company to do well in the future, signaling other investors to get in on the action.

The example of fossil-fuel *divestment* shows just how powerful shareholders can be. A study at the University of Waterloo analyzed the stock prices of 200 publicly traded fossil fuel companies. They mapped the stock price with 20 announcements of divestment from fossil fuel investments by people like Desmond Tutu and institutional investors like Stanford University's Endowment and the Rockefeller Foundation. Stock prices dropped the day of the announcements.

The practice of divesting from fossil fuel companies is ramping up. Cities like Berlin, Sydney, and even New York's $189 billion pension fund are divesting from fossil fuel companies. In 2018, Ireland became the first country to formally divest from fossil fuels. Doctors are divesting through the American Medical Association (AMA) and even Pope Francis has urged faith-based organizations to divest. **In total, $6 trillion of institutional investment is committed to divesting from fossil fuel company ownership.** These intangible actions are causing

---

[60] Pretty weird that $30 trillion is tied to our desires, huh?

companies to shift their strategies (though some are still just throwing money at climate change denial. Goodnight to you!).

The same signals support companies doing the right thing. The ETHO Climate Leadership ETF (ETHO) invests in companies that are leaders in climate impact measured by greenhouse gas emissions. Research has shown that companies who are more carbon efficient perform better than non-carbon efficient companies. The companies in the ETF produce 85% fewer carbon emissions than the collective S&P 500 companies.

Another signal for social change can happen by supporting companies with leading diversity, inclusion, and equity practices (discussed in the Diversity, Inclusion, and Equity Investing chapter). For example, the Gender Diversity ETF (SHE) and the Ellevate Global Women's Leadership fund (PXWEX) have a combined $652 million invested in these funds.

When you become an investor, you become an owner, which means you get to vote. In Madison, Wisconsin a group of shareholders in the local energy company, Madison Gas & Electric (MGE), took action and created 8 shareholder resolutions designed to nudge the company toward more environmentally-friendly policies. The company took notice and met with the activist-shareholder group, addressing many of their concerns. Companies send out resolutions for votes every year and one platform, OpenInvest, will send you the resolutions for the companies you own directly in the app, allowing you to vote on important social and environmental decisions.

Taking Action

If you review your current investments, chances are you'll find companies that don't share your values. Companies supplying oil pipelines, manufacturing and selling semi-automatic weapons and ballistic missiles, contributing dark money to political campaigns, and exploiting workers in shady supply chains. Technically, you're an owner, which means your complicit.[61]

The good news is you can own high-performing companies that are good stewards of your money and care about the things you care about. In this chapter, you'll see dozens of options for investing in these companies and responsible and profitably growing your money.

---

[61] It hurts, but it's true.

Stock Markets & Fire Swamps

If there were a cinematic depiction of the what it's like to navigate the stock market, it would be the dreaded *Fire Swamps* in *The Princess Bride*. Our dashing Westley must keep his dearly beloved Buttercup safe as they're attacked by blood-thirsty *Rodents of Unusual Size*, swallowed by *Lightning Sand*, and nearly engulfed by *Flame Spurts*.[62] If this sounds intimidating, I put together a Stock Market Primer for you in Part 3 that will share all the essentials of stock market investing, like:

- Why mutual funds suck
- How fees will kill your returns
- How to create a level playing field
- What diversification actually means
- How to determine goals, timeline, and risk

Investments Ahead

ETFs & Index Funds | Diversified funds with social and environmental benefits.

Mutual Funds | Mutual funds with uniquely low fees or sustainable and equitable investing strategies.

Individual Companies | A brief discussion of investing in sustainable, individual companies.

ETFs & Index Funds

If you haven't heard, *indexing* is the new black.

ETFs (exchange-traded funds) and Index Funds are wide basket of stock with relatively low fees.[63] Experienced investors know that *diversification* and *low fees* are two of the secrets to successful long-term investing, and investing

---

[62] If you knew what I knew, this wouldn't seem like an exaggeration.
[63] ETFs and Index Funds are nearly synonymous. The differences won't impact the typical everyday investor.

in ETFs and index funds allows you to do just that.[64] Not to mention, mutual funds with high fees are unethical, so do yourself a favor and switch over.

One of the more popular index funds in the Vanguard 500 (VFINX). When you buy a share of VFINX in your brokerage account or 401k, you get a piece of 500 of the largest U.S. companies. The problem with owning VFINX is you bolster many companies that don't share your values. Let's look at some do-gooder style index funds and ETFs.

Greening Your Funds

You can group do-gooder funds into three major themes: ESG, Fossil Fuel Free, and Renewable Energy.

ESG | ESG stands for Environmental, Social, and corporate Governance. ESG is a general indicator of how well-rounded a company is on things that matter. ESG funds typically invest in companies that score the highest on environmental and social indicators. Some funds focus on a specific area of importance, like the SPDR® SSGA Gender Diversity ETF, which invests in companies that champion advancing women.

Fossil Fuel-Free / Low-Carbon | These funds invest in companies with either a) low carbon emissions relative to their industry or b) simply exclude fossil-fuel producing corporations.

Renewable Energy | These funds invest in companies that derive revenue from renewable and/or clean energy.

Note: The table at the end of this chapter summarizes all the funds mentioned. There is a comprehensive spreadsheet with more details and sorting ability can be found at: www.adrianreif.com/dogoodersguide

---

[64] The stock market primer in Part 3 explains why hidden fees in your funds will not only erode your returns, they may be unethical.

Research Methods

One advantage of analyzing stock market investments is the plethora of information available. Every public company must report their quarterly and yearly financial results.

The increase in demand for sustainable investing also means an increase in sustainability analysis. Several companies provide in-depth research on publicly traded stocks' sustainability performance. JUST Capital, Dow Jones Sustainability Index, and Morningstar do just this.

In the following pages, the sustainability rating is represented by the **Morningstar Sustainability Rating** given to each company by Morningstar, a leading research firm. Morningstar partnered with Sustainalytics, a leading ESG research provider, to calculate the ESG score of each company in a given fund. The methodology—which is available to the public on their site—scores companies for preparedness, disclosure, and performance. Points are deducted based on a controversy score, which is triggered by incidents that have negative impact on the environment or society and pose a risk to the company itself. The final score is distributed on a scale from one to five, with five being the highest 10% of ESG performers.

Exhibit 5 Morningstar Sustainability Rating

Distribution	Score	Descriptive Rank	Rating Icon
Highest 10%	5	High	
Next 22.5%	4	Above Average	
Next 35%	3	Average	
Next 22.5%	2	Below Average	
Lowest 10%	1	Low	

ESG Funds

These funds contain companies that have been rated highly on general environmental, social, and governance (ESG) scores.

Vanguard FTSE Social Index (VFTSX) | This fund screens out the low performing companies measured on 300 environmental, social, and corporate governance indicators. These measurements look at water use, pollution, labor standards, health and safety records, and community impact, among other things.

Firms involved in coal, tobacco, weapons systems, components for controversial weapons (chemical weapons or landmines, say), are automatically excluded from the fund.

The screens kick out the worst actors. As a result, the fund's portfolio consists of 444 mostly large-company stocks. The fund's top holdings include Apple, Microsoft and Johnson & Johnson.

This fund has been around since 2000, and from January 2008 to October 2018, it grew 117%, outperforming its benchmark, the Russell 1000, which grew 107%. The S&P 500 grew 99%. The low fees (0.18%) and broad diversification make this a top choice for do-gooders. The minimum investment is $3,000.

SPDR® SSGA Gender Diversity ETF (SHE) | This fund seeks to track the performance of companies that are leaders in advancing women through gender diversity on their board of directors and in management.

Goldman Sachs JUST U.S. Large Cap Equity ETF (JUST) | Invests in 500 companies that are the *top 50%* based on corporate behavior like how they treat their employees, customer concerns, beneficial products, and job creation.

Vanguard ESG U.S. Stock ETF (ESGV) | Launched in September 2018 as a low-cost, ultra-diversified option for social investors. It *excludes* the stocks of companies producing adult entertainment, alcohol and tobacco products, conventional and controversial weapons (including civilian firearms), fossil fuels, gambling activities, and nuclear power.

The fund also excludes the stocks of companies that do not meet certain diversity criteria, as well as the labor, human rights, anti-corruption, and environmental standards defined by the Ten Principles of the United Nations Global Compact. It invests in 1,250 different stocks.

iShares MSCI USA ESG Select ETF (SUSA) | Screens out companies seen as ethically or morally questionable.

iShares MSCI KLD 400 Social ETF (DSI) | Invests in companies that have "positive environmental, social, and governance characteristics." It has been around since 2006 and invests in over 400 companies, mainly large and very-large companies, so don't expect too many surprises.

SerenityShares Impact ETF (ICAN) | Screens out tobacco, firearms, gambling and then reviews all remaining companies to identify firms whose activities have a direct, beneficial impact that addresses the societal, social, or environmental challenges. While its top holdings are Google, Apple, Facebook, and Disney, this ETF also invests in several renewable energy companies.

Vanguard ESG International Stock ETF (VSGX) | This fund uses the same screens as ESGV above, but invests in international (non-U.S.) companies. It holds 1,720 companies, providing ultra-diversification.

Fossil-Fuel Free / Low Carbon Funds

These funds invest in companies with either **a) low carbon emissions relative to their industry** or **b) exclude fossil-fuel producing corporations.**

Learn more from sites like www.gofossilfree.org and www.fossilfreefunds.org.

iShares MSCI ACWI Low Carbon Target ETF (CRBN) | This fund invests in companies with *"lower carbon exposure than that of the broad market."* This means companies with naturally lower energy needs or companies that actively manage and lower their carbon emissions. It invests in over 1,200 companies. Another similar fund is the SPDR® MSCI ACWI Low Carbon Target ETF (LOWC).

SPDR® S&P 500 Fossil Fuel Free ETF (SPYX) | Launched in 2015 with the goal of mimicking the S&P 500 *minus companies that hold fossil fuel reserves.* The investment thesis states companies with fossil fuel reserves are in for a tough future.

Change Finance Fossil Fuel Free ETF (CHGX) | This fund starts its filter with the largest 1,000 U.S. companies and then excludes companies in oil, gas, coal or tobacco; companies that produce fossil fuels; utilities that burn fossil fuels; nuclear power; and controversial human rights practices.

ETHO Climate Leadership ETF (ETHO) | Invests in companies that are leaders in "carbon impact," which is measured by greenhouse gas emissions. This fund's strategy is based on research that shows companies who are more carbon efficient perform better than non-carbon efficient companies. The total of the companies in the Etho Climate Leadership Index have 85% fewer carbon emissions than the S&P 500.

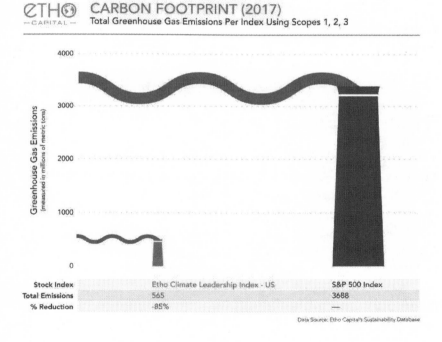

ETHO CARBON FOOTPRINT (2017)
Total Greenhouse Gas Emissions Per Index Using Scopes 1, 2, 3

Stock Index	Etho Climate Leadership Index - US	S&P 500 Index
Total Emissions	565	3688
% Reduction	-85%	—

Data Source: Etho Capital's Sustainability Database

Renewable Energy Funds

These funds invest in **companies that derive revenue from renewable and/or clean energy.**

Guggenheim Solar ETF (TAN) invests in companies involved in all solar technologies including crystalline and thin-film photovoltaic, the solar supply chain like solar farms and manufacturers, and inverters. This fund tracks an industry where predictions call for $4 trillion in new global electricity generation by 2030 to meet demand. With the cost of electricity from solar now lower than nuclear and coal, the solar industry is expected to grow.

The downside is the fund only invests in 25 companies, making it less diversified than a typical ETF. If one or two of those companies do poorly, the entire fund could suffer. For higher risk tolerant investors.

The PowerShares WilderHill Clean Energy Portfolio (PBW) | Invests in U.S. companies that are in the business of cleaner energy or energy conservation. For example, the fund holds CREE, an LED lighting company.

First Trust ISE Global Wind Energy Index Fund (FAN) | Invests 67% of its fund in companies that provide goods and services exclusively to the wind energy industry. The companies are spread across the globe, giving you exposure to Spain, Germany, Denmark, and China wind markets. However, it only holds 46 companies and as such, can be volatile.

Renewable Energy YieldCos

YieldCos are an easy way for the everyday stock market investor to invest in renewable energy.

YieldCos own renewable energy production facilities. They trade on the stock market like a stock, but they also pay out consistent dividends. The average dividend yield of listed YieldCos was 6.2% in 2016, with a range of 3%-15%. YieldCos are explained in-depth in the Renewable Energy chapter.

Mutual Funds

Mutual funds are similar to index funds in that they invest in a wide variety of stocks, but mutual funds have come under fire because they often have hidden fees that can eat into the growth of your money.

Here is a list of sustainable mutual funds that are unique because of a) low fees or b) a specific investing strategy.

PAX Ellevate Global Women's Leadership (PXWEX) | Invests in the highest rated companies in the world for advancing women through gender diversity on their boards and in executive management. Fees are a bit high (0.80%), but many investors support it.

Aspiration Redwood Fund (REDWX) | Aspiration's platform simplifies responsible saving and investing for the everyday investor. This fund has no hidden fees, a modest expense ratio (0.50%), and has one of the highest sustainability ratings among mutual funds.

Domini Impact Bond Fund (DSBFX) | A unique fund that invests in socially-responsible bonds as well as affordable housing and small business development. Its expense ratio is 1.11%, making this fund a tough sell.

Individual Companies

While indexing is the way to go, some investors still love the thrill of picking a good stock.

When I started investing 16 years ago, trying to find the next rocketship company was more fun than playing Donkey Kong. I'm happy to boast about earning 1000% on Whole Foods Market stock. Or the 800% return on Vestas Wind Energy. *Cha-ching*. But I most certainly *won't* tell you about the time I lost *all the money* I invested in China Electric Motors.[65]

I've pulled way back on investing in individual stocks, opting to focus my energy on the *all-weather, long-term strategies* featured in Part 3.

---

[65] I thought I would make it rich on this stock, didn't do enough research beforehand, and felt the pain of the gamble when the company went out of business.

Despite the caution, many readers will want to try their hand at picking stocks. So, I put together a list of some of the most sustainable corporations based on ESG, use of renewable energy, water responsibility, and development of green technology. To save paper, the complete list is at www.adrianreif.com/stocks.

401K PLANS

If you offer 401K or other retirement plans for your employees, Social K is the leading provider of sustainable retirement plans. Social K has been around for 15 years and has invested over $150 million on behalf of their clients. They are a Certified B Corp and donate to 1% For The Planet.

A More Sustainable
Stock Market—Review

As you plan for your future, investing in a more sustainable stock market can help you grow your money.

- Deutsche-Bank analyzed 2,000 empirical studies from 1970s to now. Ninety-percent of the studies showed that sustainably-focused investing provided higher returns than passive investing.
- An investment in a public company is a vote with your investment dollar.
- Using low-cost ETFs and index funds, you can invest in companies with high environmental, social, and governance (ESG) scores.
- You can support women's advancement in the workplace with a gender diversity ETF.
- YieldCos are a great way to invest in diversified renewable energy companies.

The table below summarizes the sustainable stock market investments mentioned in this chapter. To see a more in-depth spreadsheet, go www.adrianreif.com/dogoodersguide.

**A target return is impossible to predict, therefore the investments are summarized by their impact score based on Morningstar's Sustainability Score when available, fees, and Morningstar % rank in category, which ranks how closely the investment has performed to other similar investments in that class.

Fund	Impact Score (Out of 5)	Morningstar % Rank In Category	Expense Ratio
USA ESG Select ETF	5	1%	0.50%
Change Finance Diversified Impact U.S. Large Cap Fossil Fuel Free ETF	5	1%	0.49%
Vanguard PRIMECAP Inv	5	1%	0.39%
Saturna Sustainable Equity	5	1%	0.75%
KLD 400 Social ETF	5	2%	0.50%
Calvert International Equity	5	2%	1.34%
Jensen Quality Growth	5	3%	0.88%
Vanguard Capital Opportunity Inv	5	4%	0.44%
Aspiration Redwood Fund	5	6%	0.51%
Green Century Balanced	5	6%	1.48%
TIAA-CREF Social Choice Low Carbon Equity	5	8%	0.32%
Parnassus Core Equity Investor	5	9%	0.87%
Vanguard FTSE Social Index	5	10%	0.20%

PAX Ellevate Global Women's Leadership	5	10%	0.80%
Gender Diversity ETF	4	15%	0.20%
iShares Edge MSCI USA Momentum Fctr ETF	4	17%	0.15%
Calvert Emerging Markets Equity	4	24%	1.27%
ETHO Climate Leadership ETF	4	25%	0.47%
New Alternatives Fund	4	32%	1.12%
S&P 500 Fossil Fuel Free ETF	4	34%	0.20%
Low Carbon Target ETF	4	45%	0.20%
SerenityShares Impact ETF	3	94%	0.50%
PowerShares WilderHill Clean Energy Portfolio	3	95%	0.70%
Appleseed Fund	1	95%	1.23%
Guggenheim Solar ETF	5	100%	0.70%
Columbia U.S. Social Bond Fund Class A	3	n/a	0.70%
Saturna Sustainable Bonds	3	n/a	0.65%
Aspiration Flagship Fund	4	n/a	1.55%
Domini Social Bond Fund	3	n/a	0.87%

Automated Investing for Good

Chances are you automate certain parts of your life. It's now easier than ever to automate investing, too, thanks to technology. The name given to these online platforms is "robo-advisors"—not to be confused with Robo Cop—because they can do some neat little tricks that a human advisor can help you do, but with less cost.

Before you jump headfirst into an automated investing platform, a word of caution: I recommend a solid grasp of the basics of investing. A robo-advisor can *sort of* customize a portfolio for you, but an algorithm selects your investments. If you don't know what your goals are, it may offer recommendations not right for you. For example, Swell Investing's "healthy living portfolio" includes Lululemon and Foot Locker, two brands I don't want to invest in because of their focus on continual consumption of new schtuff. Had I not been paying attention, those companies would have become part of my portfolio. The same goes for Motif, which placed Wells Fargo and British American Tobacco in a "customized" Sustainable Planet portfolio. I mentioned my reasons for choosing to not bank with Wells Fargo in the Banking for Good chapter.

The good news is when you have a clear understanding of your investment needs—risk tolerance, goals, values, and potential asset allocation (see Part 3)—an automated investing platform can help you keep fees low, rebalance your portfolio every year (which keeps you in alignment with your target allocation), and sometimes type in certain cheat codes to help you lower taxes. A few of these platforms allow you to have 100% control over each investment, which I highly recommend.

If these services sound intriguing, you can often create a free account and build a "customized" portfolio recommended by their algorithms. If you are particular about what you want to own, go through the recommendations and see how they line up with your values. This will not only ensure the service will be valuable, it will make you a better investor.

Here's a look at five platforms that could help you automate and simplify your sustainable investing. *Note: I left out platforms like Betterment and

Wealthfront, two of the common mainstream platforms, because they do not have a particular focus on sustainable investing, though they may now have some sustainable "options." The platforms below are listed in my order of preference, with clear statements where each platform falls short.

Investment Platforms Ahead

OpenInvest | A progressive, impact-focused platform that lets you build a fully customizable values-aligned portfolio.

EarthFolio | An established platform with great backtesting, transparency, and commitment to responsible investing.

Aspiration | A streamlined platform with a checking account attached that makes it very easy to get started investing in two unique, well-constructed, low-fee mutual funds.

Swell Investing | Six grab-and-go portfolios that represent renewable energy, clean water, and other impact themes. Portfolios need some work.

Motif | A low-fee platform that allows customized portfolio, with a minimal focus on true sustainability.

OpenInvest

OpenInvest is the most progressive, impact-focused automated investing platform. Like other services, OpenInvest learns what causes you care about and builds a recommended portfolio. However, OpenInvest creates a personalized mutual fund for you that *only holds the companies you want to invest in*, instead of investing in existing mutual funds. You can invest via your values by choosing themes like:

- Divest from Dark Money,
- Divest from Deforestation,
- Divest from Gun Violence,
- Invest in Pro-LGBTQ Companies,
- Invest in Women in the Workplace and more.

A powerful tool OpenInvest provides is easy shareholder voting—the OpenInvest app pushes every shareholder ballot measure to your phone, so you can vote. For example, if you are an Apple shareholder, you can vote on whether Apple should have a human rights committee oversee their company policies.

Features: Flat fee, No trading fees, Auto rebalancing
Advantages: Fee covers everything (since there are no ETF expense ratios), Most customizable based on values
Drawbacks: Existing ETFs are not available, taking many great options off the board
Cost: 0.50% annual fee
Minimum Investment: $100

EarthFolio

The longest-running platform, EarthFolio helps you invest sustainably in the stock market. Their software analyzes your current investments, assesses your financial needs and sustainability goals, and recommends a portfolio of low-cost mutual funds for you. EarthFolio even back-tests their recommended investments so you can see how they've performed over the last 15 years. You can link your current brokerage account for analysis and compare it to their recommended asset allocation.

Features: Free trading, No-load mutual funds, Free rebalancing
Advantage: Long history, deep sustainable focus
Drawbacks: Chooses mutual funds (which have higher internal fees)
Cost: 0.50% annual fee
Minimum Investment: $25,000

Aspiration

Aspiration simplifies investing. Through an online account, you can invest in two low-fee mutual funds: The Redwood Fund (REDWX) and the Flagship Fund (ASPFX).

The Flagship Fund is a unique offering that provides "one-stop" access to a range of strategies once out of reach to everyday investors. The goal of this fund is to grow your money steadily over the long-term while trying to reduce the amount of ups and downs of the stock market along the way. The Flagship Fund is unique in that it seeks "alternative strategies," which can be more sophisticated than investing in companies' stocks.[66]

The Redwood Fund is a fund that owns a broad range of large companies that score well on ESG criteria.

Features: Two straightforward fund options, High-yield savings account, Low-fees
Advantages: Access to alternative strategies that are less volatile through the Flagship Fund
Drawbacks: Lack of customization, No automatic rebalancing
Cost: 0.50%-1.33% expense ratio for mutual funds; Free checking account
Minimum Investment: $100

Swell Investing

Swell Investing offers six grab-and-go portfolios like Renewable Energy, Clean Water, or Disease Eradication. Like OpenInvest, Swell's portfolios are a personalized mutual fund that includes annual rebalancing.

Swell's heart is in the right place, but the challenge of aligning investments and impact remains. For example, the "Healthy Living Portfolio" invests in

---

[66] Alternative strategies might include open-end funds, ETFs, and closed-end funds that emphasize alternative strategies, such as funds that sell securities short; employ asset allocation, managed futures, arbitrage and/or option-hedged strategies; or that invest in distressed securities, the natural resources sector and business development companies. Phew, if you made it this far, congrats!

consumption-focused luxury brands like Lululemon and Foot Locker. On the outside, Lululemon and Foot Locker may symbolize active lifestyles, but let's be honest, these companies really want to sell more clothes.

Features: No trading fees, Auto rebalancing
Advantages: 100% customization available
Drawbacks: You'll need to do a lot of your own research to really build a values-aligned, profitable portfolio; Highest annual fee
Cost: 0.75% annual fee
Minimum Investment: $50

Motif

Motif—pronounced Mo' teef—offers several "impact" portfolios, but the only real selling point is the low 0.25% fee. For the truly sustainable-minded investor, Motif has some challenges to overcome. For example, when Motif built a Sustainable Planet "personalized investment plan" for me, the stocks included Scotts Miracle-Gro, Wells Fargo, and British American Tobacco. An investor who doesn't look deeper wouldn't know Scotts Miracle-Gro owns the brand RoundUp, a controversial and likely dangerous herbicide. Wells Fargo is a major funder of the Dakota Access Pipeline. And British American Tobacco sells $20 billion worth of cigarettes around the world and is involved in corruption in several African countries.

Features: Low fees
Advantages: Customizable
Drawbacks: Not much effort put in to sustainable portfolio starting points
Fee: 0.25%
Minimum Investment: $1,000

Automated Investing for Good—Review

Once you have solid understanding of investing and the direction you're want to go, using a robo-advisor to select and rebalance your investments can save you time.

- Robo-advisors "personalized" portfolios are built by algorithms, making them decent starting points for a portfolio, but rarely should they have the final say.
- Benefits of automated investing platforms include reasonable "advisory" fees, automatic rebalancing, and sometimes tax-loss harvesting.
- OpenInvest and EarthFolio are the top two robo-advisors that can help you create meaningful, well-constructed portfolios.
- Aspiration offers two unique, one-stop mutual funds.
- Swell Investing and Motif provide poor screens for their investment recommendations.

Platform	Cost	Min. Invest	Advantages
OpenInvest	0.50%	$100	Strong screens, Shareholder voting
EarthFolio	0.50%	$25,000	Focus on sustainable investing
Aspiration	0.50%-1.33%	$100	Alternative strategies fund
Swell	0.75%	$50	No trading fees
Motif	0.25%	$1,000	Lowest fees

Crowdfunding & Angel Investing

"Entrepreneurs are the drivers of our economy—the innovators, the dreamers, the ones crazy enough to create something from nothing and potentially change the world. By backing them, you can make a difference too."[67]

Words to my heart. As an entrepreneur and investor, there's nothing that excites me more than a bold new idea racing to build a better world.

In 2016, I made my first angel investment. I'd spent several weeks learning more about **SONDORS** Electric Car. If I were fancy I'd call it *due diligence*. I researched their history, read up on the founder, and compared their vision for the future with my own. Everything was a match. I still felt trepidation as I typed my investment amount into the box on the crowdfunding website, cursor hovering over the "Invest" box. While I believed in the company, I knew it was *possible* I'd lose the money I put in. *Probably*, I should say, having been an entrepreneur and knowing just how hard it is out there. I clicked "Invest" anyway. Please don't tell my wife.[68]

I joined 1,300 other investors who collectively placed $1 million of money—and faith—in this innovative, young company. All of us hope SONDORS's affordable electric car sells beyond expectations and we all get a nice, fat check someday.

For investors with the desire and risk tolerance, angel investing opens a channel to growing your money—and creating impact. If it's not clear yet, angel investing is like, oh, gambling. You think you have expertise that leads to financial reward, but in reality, luck drives the ship. I'm drawn to angel investing for another reason—I want to see companies do the unthinkable. Affordable electric cars. Clean water for everyone. Blockchain access for rural Africans.

---

[67] From SeedInvest.com

[68] In all seriousness, discuss investing with your partner and make sure you're on the same page. It's likely you don't have the same risk tolerances and we don't want this causing any trouble, especially over a little money.

Let's take a quick look at angel investing and the burgeoning world of equity crowdfunding—and how you can participate in building a world you want to see.

Angel Investing vs. Equity Crowdfunding

For the sake of this book, let's consider angel investing and equity crowdfunding as the same. Traditionally, an angel investor was a high-net-worth (HNW) individual who invested early in a company's lifecycle with amounts ranging from $10,000 to $250,000 (generally speaking, as there are no real boundaries).

Crowdfunding is relatively new, thanks to the JOBS act, and makes it easier for everyday people to find young companies seeking capital. One distinguishable feature between angel investing and crowdfunding is the dollar amount, with angel investing usually indicating higher dollar amounts of investment, while crowdfunding typically represents smaller amounts—under $10,000 per year. Crowdfunding is also done through a registered online crowdfunding platform, like the ones mentioned ahead, although many angel investors now find companies through these platforms as well.

The Rise of the Crowd

In 2012, the U.S. tippy-toed closer to its meritocratic ideals thanks to the passing of the Jumpstart our Business Startups— or JOBS—Act. In 2015, the SEC[69] finally published the rules that would govern "non-accredited"—aka everyday investors—and how they were able to invest.

Before the JOBS Act, the SEC's rules only allowed accredited investors to angel invest in private companies, intending to keep unsuspecting investors like us from getting scammed or losing more money than we could afford. While the intention was noble, it made sure accredited investors made the decisions on which new companies got funded.

Innovation demands better. A country is far more innovative when more people, who are more diverse, bring more ideas to the table. Since equity crowdfunding has emerged, an additional hundreds of millions of

---

[69] The Securities and Exchange Commission, not the Southeastern Conference. Go Dores!

dollars has flowed into small businesses and start-ups.[70] There haven't been any overnight everyday millionaires from crowdfunding, and this is a good thing. Real innovation demands "patient capital." Plus, we've seen plenty of bursted bubbles thanks to supposedly savvy venture capitalists and accredited investors. Might crowdfunding be the start of a march up Mount Doom to destroy Sauron's reign of power?[71]

Rewards vs Equity

Rewards crowdfunding—like Kickstarter or Indiegogo—is not to be confused with *equity* crowdfunding. Kickstarter *is* awesome—perfect for grabbing the latest travel dress with 15 pockets or supporting artists. Equity crowdfunding, on the other hand, not only allows you to give a vote of confidence to a company, you get a small ownership stake in the company's future financial success.

In 2012, Oculus Rift sparked a big debate over which one is better. When they launched their "immersive" gaming VR headset on Kickstarter over 9,000 contributors *backed* the project, helping Oculus raise a ripe $2.4 million. If you had invested $1,000 in Oculus it would have been worth $400,000. Since the project was a rewards crowdfunding project, Oculus Rift delivered t-shirts and headsets to their eager backers. Everybody was happy. Two years later, Facebook purchased the company for $2 billion. A debate ensued. Should those 9,000 contributors who brought Oculus Rift to life reaped some rewards during the massive wealth creation from the sale of the company? Of course, Oculus Rift did nothing wrong. They didn't know a $2 billion sale was around the corner. Had those 9,000 backers invested, they could just have easily lost their money if Oculus had gone out of business. For now, the debate has settled down. Most people know if they just want a cool product, or if they want to take a big risk on a startup.

---

[70] While everyone *can* invest, not everyone *should*.

[71] Am I likening Sauron to venture capitalists? (If you don't know who Sauron is, he's the near-infinitely powerful bad guy in Lord of the Rings. Younger people can substitute Thanos with all the stones.) Back to venture capitalists....They don't call them "vulture capitalists" without reason. No, I am not saying that venture capitalists, banks, and hedge funds are *evil*! I don't want to hurt their feelings. But, when they align their incentives with maximizing profit, they will inherently lose sight of what's best for humanity as a whole. If you're really torn by this "anti-capitalist" sentiment, call me and we can talk it out.

How to Make Money

Angel investing is exciting, but every great angel investor needs to know how they're going to make their money back. (Have I mentioned how risky angel investing can be?)

An exit | An "exit" is when a company is purchased by a bigger company. If the purchase price is big enough, early investors could get paid for their ownership.

Since crowdfunding is still young, there haven't been many noteworthy exits from crowdfunding companies. There have been several in the U.K. and Israel. In the U.K., BrewDog, a craft brewery operator, used crowdfunding early on in their expansion. When they sold a 23% stake in the company to a private equity firm, the earliest investors earned 2,800% on their investment.

Go public | Startup investors can make money when a company goes public. Similar to an exit above, an IPO—or initial public offering—sells shares in the company to the public on a stock exchange. Typically the value of the company is greater than when early investors invested.

In 2016, Elio Motors raised $16 million from everyday investors on StartEngine (featured ahead) to build its 84 MPG car. The company went public on a small stock exchange. Since the company was hot, the share price quadrupled until coming back down to near initial offering prices. Early investors who sold at the peak earned 400%.

Fixed Return | Like many of the fixed return (aka fixed income) investments featured in this book, some crowdfunding sites offer investment options that provide a more consistent payout. These investment terms include: *revenue sharing agreements, loans, and dividends,* and are less reliant on a big exit to pay you a return.

LocalStake and NextSeed offer investment deals for local companies that promise a 50%-100% payback (usually over 2-5 years). Other investments like those listed on Abundance Investments (in the U.K.) offer deals in renewable energy and affordable housing projects with 4%-12% returns per year.

Secondary Market | In the scenarios above, you have to wait on the company to sell or go public to earn any money. A secondary market is a marketplace of buyers and sellers for crowdfunded companies, where investors can go to sell or buy shares without waiting for the company to exit. It's like a small stock market and will help to provide liquidity to everyday angel investors. There are a few secondary markets in development in the U.S., but the only active secondary crowdfunding market is Seedrs in the U.K.

9 Investing Strategies From the World's Best Investors

I like to surround myself with people smarter than I am. Before you take the plunge, take a look at investing advice from some of the best investors in the world:

1. Invest in companies that have already built their product.

Billionaire venture capitalist Chris Sacca, who invested early in Twitter and Uber—but missed out on AirBnB because he thought it was dangerous—always invests in companies that have already built their product, or a strong prototype.

2. Test the product.

Famous stock market investor Peter Lynch would look for products he and his family loved before investing. See if you *love* it. If you do, chances are a lot of other people will, too.

3. Develop your own thesis.

Before you start investing, develop your own decision-making criteria up front. For example, some investors believe cloud computing is the next disruption, so they only invest in companies that could benefit from cloud computing. Other only invest in specific sectors that they know really well and have "inside information" about. This will help you stay disciplined and avoid shiny-object syndrome.

4. Invest in People.

It's easy to get excited about an idea, but experienced investors know ideas are only as valuable as their execution. Get to know the team. Talk with the CEO. Most crowdfunding platforms host live Q&A webinars with company CEOs. Does their past experience stand up to the vision they are pitching now?

5. The company must have cash for 12 months.

Finland's wunderkind investor Kim Väisänen invests mostly with intuition, but says a company should have at least 12 months worth of cash on hand after the fundraise, otherwise they'll be focused on raising capital and not on building the best product.

6. Be a diligence shark.

Shark Tank's sharks like Damon John and Mark Cuban want to know everything they can about a company before they invest. Often times their offer to invest on the show is only validated after the company passes additional due diligence. While raising funds, a company must provide a lot of information, including past financials, projections, backgrounds on their team, and more. Do your due diligence so you're not surprised later.

7. Hold for the long term.

Warren Buffet doesn't get too excited when the market goes up or down. As I like to say: "Invest and chill." Don't expect to get rich quick—or at all. Expect to support the company and watch them grow over time.

8. Invest alongside smart people.

While not guaranteed to make you money, investing alongside experienced investors can be insightful, cut the costs of due diligence, and offer fun people to be around, especially when *do-gooder* investing is the topic. The end of the chapter features several angel investing communities for impact investors.

9. Never invest more than you can afford to lose.

Consider the investment like a social good lottery ticket.

Crowdfunding Rules & Limits for Non-Accredited Investors

For every 12 month period:
- Everyone can invest at least $2,000
- If *either* your net worth or income are below $107k, you may legally invest a maximum of 5% of the *lesser* number. ($5,000 if you make $100,000)
- If *both* your net worth or income are above $107k, you may legally invest a maximum of 10% of the *lesser* number. ($11,000 if you make $110,000)
- No one, including accredited investors, may invest more than $107,000 in Regulation Crowdfunding deals per year.

Crowdfunding Platforms Ahead

Everyday investors who want to participate in angel investing can find investments in young companies via certified, regulated platforms. Here are the top six platforms where you can find sustainable or local investments.[72]

StartEngine | A leading equity crowdfunding platform with a secondary market in the works.

Republic | A crowdfunding platform with a focus on founder diversity and mission-driven startups.

SeedInvest | Hosts deals for both accredited and non-accredited investors and features an *automated investing* option—like a mutual fund for startups.

Wefunder | As a *Public Benefit Corporation*, Wefunder is on a mission to share the rewards of capitalism more broadly.

---

[72] Note: You can also use the platforms featured in the Local Investing chapter to find deals, too.

LocalStake | Features small, local businesses that are raising money through revenue share loans, preferred equity, and traditional loans.

NextSeed | Hosts fixed-income deals from brick and mortar businesses with 50% to 150% target returns.

Impact Investing Communities | A list of *do-gooder* angel investor networks where you can learn from experienced investors and invest together.

Adrian's Aside: Putting My Money Where My Mouth—and Lungs—Are

I like clean air. I also see huge potential in the electrification of cars. In Shenzhen, one of China's biggest cities, the public bus fleet is already 100% electric.

With the industry cruising along, I believe there's big money to be made while helping people around the planet breath easier. So I became one of 1,300 investors that helped SONDORS Electric Car raise its first $1 million.

The company's founder, Storm Sondors, likes clean air so much he founded Sondors Premium Electric Bikes in 2015. Storm crowdfunded the early stages of the bike company, which has become the largest electric bike distributor in the U.S.

While SONDORS makes cool cars and will do remarkably well, I invested another reason. I'm tired of the status quo. If you take a hard look at the state of automobiles, it's nothing but status quo. Gas mileage has wallowed as automotive CEOs focus on stock prices instead of innovation. Case in point: the U.S. automotive fleet's fuel economy went from 16.9 miles per gallon in 1991 to a whopping 17.2 mpg over a decade later. Yet, we hold up these "titans of industry" like they've landed on the moon.

Car prices continue to rise. Gas bills cut deeper into paychecks. And with more cars on the road, air pollution has become an early Grim Reaper for millions of people around the world.

Instead of standing on the sidelines, Storm Sondors made a decision. He decided the time had come to radically disrupt the automotive world. If Detroit wasn't going to do it, who was?

The SONDORS Vision

SONDORS is building an electric car priced at $15,000. The car's sleek design and minimalism help it drive efficiently while costing less. SONDORS's fleet of electric cars could replace clunkers, slash gas bills, and reduce air pollution.

Traditionally, a deal like this would rely on investment bankers and venture capital firms, making the cost to raise capital exorbitant.

Since raising their first $1 millions, SONDORS has already raised another round of capital from the crowd and rolled out a drivable prototype.

Will the SONDORS EV save the world? No. They may not even succeed.

But if we're going to build a better world, we need thousands of SONDORS tackling challenges from transportation, affordable housing, pollution, equality, and more. And we need do-gooders like you there to invest in them.

StartEngine

StartEngine has facilitated $100 million in equity investment into young companies since 2015. They even have a Secondary Market—like a small stock market—in beta where you can sell your shares after the initial deal.[73] In 2018, you could even invest in StartEngine itself.

StartEngine is unique among crowdfunding platforms because it only hosts investments open to everyday investors.

Some of the companies funded through StartEngine:
- Elio Motors—A $7,000, 84 MPG car
- SONDORS Electric Car—A $15,000 electric car
- Kind Katie Movies—Faith-based films
- Buying Collective—A clean, affordable food company
- PlantSnap—Plant identification app
- Biotech Restorations—Restores polluted lands
- 4-Scored—Hotel investment company
- Farm.One—Vertical urban farming

My favorite investment | Red Mountain, a top-rated ski mountain in Canada. Yes, you could have been part owner of a world-class ski resort.

Republic

Republic is crowdfunding's freshest player. They add a focus on diversity and mission-driven start-ups, with the view that equalization of the fundraising landscape will allow more talent a chance to build companies.

The investment industry scores low on diversity, with only 13% of CEOs backed by venture capital firms being underrepresented founders of color, 3% being women, and 57% going to the state of California.

---

[73] Some deals require a year before shares can be listed on the secondary market.

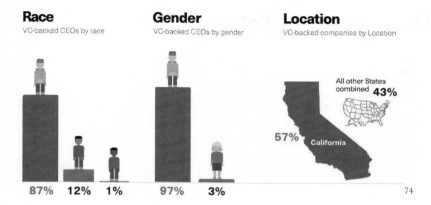

Race
VC-backed CEOs by race

Gender
VC-backed CEOs by gender

Location
VC-backed companies by Location

All other States combined **43%**

57% California

87%   12%   1%   97%   3%   74

In 2018, Republic's *Diversity Report* noted that 25% of investments via Republic have gone "to companies with underrepresented founders of color and 44% have gone to companies with a female founder versus 1% and 13%, respectively, for the industry."

Twenty-two percent of US angel investors are women. On Republic, 30% of investors have been female. About 8% of venture capital partners are women.

Republic's platform allows investors to see if startups are started by veterans, black founders, women founders, immigrant founders, or focus on social and environmental impact.

A few companies funded on Republic include:
- Farm from a Box—Off-grid technology for agriculture
- Coinvest—A cryptocurrency index fund
- Everytable—Fresh, healthy, affordable fast food
- Phluid—World's first gender-free clothing store
- Geostellar—National solar installer

---

[74] Source: Republic.co

SeedInvest

Since its inception, SeedInvest has helped investors fund 150+ companies receiving $95 million in investment. SeedInvest features both deals for accredited and non-accredited everyday investors.

One feature that helps SeedInvest standout from the crowdfunding crowd is an Automated Investing option. This mutual fund for startups lets you invest in 25 companies with one investment.

If you want to go in deeper on angel investing, check out SeedInvest's Crowdfunding Academy, which houses 17 guides for learning more about investing, with topics like "How to Manage a Portfolio of Startup Investments" and "The Language of Crowdfunding."

A sample of companies funded through SeedInvest:
- Virtuix—Immersive VR gaming
- Knightscope—Autonomous security robots
- HelloMD—The Amazon of cannabis
- Blokable—High-performance modular homes
- Patch of Land—Real estate crowdfunding

Wefunder

Wefunder's mission is to increase economic growth and lower wealth disparity by sharing the rewards of capitalism more broadly. Wefunder even makes a commitment to help immigrants, minorities, and the poor find access to funding. Since inception, 130,000+ investors have invested $54 million in companies raising capital through Wefunder. Wefunder is a Public Benefit Corporation, a new legal structure that embeds a legal obligation to benefit society into their business model.

According to Wefunder: **"Changing the world is hard; most startups die. But by funding more founders who strive valiantly to take their shot, we enrich our society and boost our talent, even if they fail."**

Wefunder Charter

Wefunder wants to see change, and their "charter" reads like a revolutionary manifesto.

1. More startups and small businesses increase the wealth of America. Young, hungry, and scrappy companies do more, faster.

2. The people are wiser than banks or venture capitalists. The "wisdom of the crowd" allocates capital better than elite gatekeepers.

3. Everyone deserves the right to invest in what they believe in. The middle class must rise up and break the monopoly of the wealthy.

4. Investing in dreams—win or lose—benefits us all.

Some of the companies funded through Wefunder:

- Ganaz—App that connects farmworkers with the best farm jobs
- Airing Inc.—The first mask-less, hoseless device for sleep apnea
- Malibu Compost —First biodynamic bagged compost
- LPP Fusion—2 billion degree fusion generator that could replace fossil fuels
- Mission Brewery—San Diego microbrew with $4M in sales in 2016

LocalStake

LocalStake hosts small businesses looking to raise money from their communities.

Unlike start-up oriented platforms, Local Stake investments can provide fixed returns through: Revenue share loans, preferred equity, or traditional loans.

Some of the companies funded through LocalStake:

- Cardinal Spirits—Craft distillery in Bloomington, IN
- Scotty's Brewhouse—12 locations, Indianapolis, IN
- King Dough—Wood-fired mobile pizza oven in Bloomington, IN
- Freshwater Fix—Real estate redevelopment in Milwaukee, WI
- Unity Vibration—Kombucha tea and beer makers in Ypsilanti, MI

NextSeed

NextSeed focuses on fixed return deals from brick and mortar businesses. Instead of receiving ownership, investors receive dividend payments neatly posted to their NextSeed account.

Most deals target a 50% return with a $100 minimum investment. These attractive returns have helped fund place-based businesses like:

- The Native—An upscale hostel in Austin, TX
- Pitch 25—Soccer bar next to Houston Dynamo stadium
- Chino Taco Bar—Next generation taco bar
- Oakland Rec Club—Hip cocktails and pool hall
- Healing Waters—Flotation therapy in Houston, TX

Impact Investing Communities

For accredited investors who want to make larger investments in social enterprises, impact investing communities bring together angel investors. The benefits for you are reduced risk, streamlined due diligence, reduced deal costs, and sharing of best practices.

Here's a look at five networks bringing do-gooder angel investors together to create impact and make money:

- Investor's Circle

- Toniic
- Transform Finance
- Investor Flow
- Social Venture Connection (SVX) - Canada

Investor's Circle

For 25 years, Investor's Circle has brought together angel investors with one goal: **"Speed up the transition to a sustainable economy by increasing investment in companies that are addressing social and environmental challenges."** Their network has propelled $172 million plus $4 billion in follow on investment into 271 social enterprises.

Standout Feature: Investor's Circle offers a diversified fund that gives investors access to multiple companies.

Toniic

Toniic members are passionate about impact investing. Members convene monthly through virtual and in-person meetings in San Francisco, Amsterdam and India to discuss deals.

Standout Feature: For investors who want to get up to speed fast, Toniic hosts a 3-day *Impact Investor Practicum* with hands-on learning for investment strategies.

Transform Finance

Transform sets itself apart from other communities because **its members are specifically dedicated to a *social justice* approach to impact investment.**

Transform focuses on community-centered investing and holds the belief that finance can be transformative for society and nature.

Standout Feature: Transform's site host several free webinars that illustrate the transformative power of finance, including, *The Movement for Black Lives and the Role of Investors, Affordable Housing Without Government Subsidies,* and *Renewable Energy Impacts on Communities.*

investorflow.org

investorflow.org pipes vetted social impact deals to specific investors through email. With 388 investors across 32 countries, investorflow.org helps put the right investors together. Sign up for free at investorflow.org.

Social Venture Connection (SVX) Canada

SVX connects Canadian angel investors with social impact companies raising money. Companies like SolarShare, Canada's largest renewable energy cooperative, and the Immigrant Access Fund have raised money on SVX.

Accredited Investors Only

Accredited investors can use the following platforms to find start-up investments, although they are not specifically focused on sustainable companies:
- AngelList
- CircleUp
- Crowdfunder
- Bolstr

Angel Investing & Crowdfunding—Review

Angel investing and equity crowdfunding allow you to invest directly into young companies building a better world, with chances of a higher return and higher impact.

- New equity crowdfunding laws allow everyday investors access to innovative, young companies, with investment limits per year.
- Your money goes right into the business, not Wall Street.
- One prominent example: SONDORS, makers of a $15,000 electric car, has raised over $2 million solely from the crowd.
- If you decide to angel invest, have a strategy and know how to make your money back.
- "9 Investing Strategies From the World's Best Investors" including test the product, develop your own thesis, and more.
- Crowdfunding is risky. Don't invest more than you can lose.
- Angel investing communities allow you to invest alongside experienced social impact investors and share investing best practices.

Investing Platform	Deals hosted	Niche
StartEngine	251	Scalable startups
SeedInvest	105	Only highly vetted startups
Wefunder	235	Scalable social enterprises
Republic.co	50	Scalable social enteprises + focus on diversity of founders
LocalStake	36	Food & beverage in Indiana and Michigan
NextSeed	33	Brick and mortar concepts, debt only

Investment Advisors

If you were an Olympic or pro athlete, you'd have a coach to help you train, recover, eat right, and likely talk to when things aren't going your way.

If you're feeling stuck in your investment game, a great advisor can help you pull together a winning strategy and guide you to a podium finish.

I started my career as an investment advisor and before you dive in, I have to be drastically honest with you—**not all advisors are created equal.**

In this chapter, I pull back the curtain on several deceptive industry practices and give you the *7 Questions You Absolutely Must Ask Your Advisor*. This will no doubt ruffle feathers in the industry, but you deserve to have a coach who's on your team.

"Pay no attention to the man behind the curtain..."

The Wizard of Oz did not want Dorothy to pull back that green curtain, but a booming god-like voice won't protect the financial advising world any longer.

How Advisors Get Paid

The first step to finding a trustworthy advisor is understanding how advisors get paid. Financial advisors get paid in three ways:

1. Commissions
2. Management fee
3. Financial planning fees

Commissions

The finance industry is still hanging on to its old school beginnings. Back in the day, advisors made their money from commissions.[75] You know, good ol' fashion *Wolf of Wall Street* style.

Commissions are small percentages—or kick-backs—paid to advisors from a mutual fund company when their client buys their mutual fund. In these old school firms advisors are glorified salesmen, working to hit monthly bonuses. You want to stay away from this.

A high-pressure sales environment and kickbacks create an unhealthy conflict of interest, tempting advisors to recommend, or *sell,* you investments that aren't right for you.

In fact, many people believe this sales-focused approach should be illegal, but the finance industry turns a healthy profit from these commissions, making it very hard to change.

The checklist at the end of the chapter will help you find advisors that don't get paid on commissions.

Fee-Only

Advisors who get paid by a management fee are often called "fee-only" advisors. The fee ranges between 0.50% and 2% of the total amount of money they manage for you—commonly called "assets under management," or AUM.

Of course, they don't manage your money without your input. So really their job is to understand you and advise accordingly. The "fee-only" payment model is more customer-friendly and creates less conflict of interest.

Financial Planning

Some advisors are paid only for financial planning consultations. Like going to the doctor for a checkup or nutritionist for a food plan, you pay your advisor for a one-off meeting where they try to understand your entire financial picture, including your specific goals and risk tolerance.

---

[75] In this case, old school means lack of progression, not the best movie of all time.

In this case, an advisor should work together with you to create a personalized financial plan. Some of the advisors I talked to like Conscious Capital Management and Natural Investments charge a reasonable *flat fee* for a planning consult. Even scrappy DIY investors can benefit from a financial planning consultation every so often, to see where they may be going wrong. The downside to a financial planning consultation is that it's up to you to execute on the plan.

Is the Cost Worth It?

Finance gurus often eschew advisors, saying the cost isn't worth it. In reality, the answer is not black and white.

To find out if an advisor is right for you, ask yourself, **"How will this advisor improve my financial life?"** If you really want to work out, but you only show up if you hire a personal trainer, chances are it's a good thing. In terms of your money, if hiring an advisor is the only way you'll put together a long-term investment strategy—when, let's be honest, you haven't yet— you may want to consider it.

If you shudder at the talk of asset allocation and could care less about rebalancing, your "hands-off" investing approach might need a little kick in the butt.

On the other hand, if you've cruised through Part 3 of this book, organized your all-weather investing strategy in a tidy Excel spreadsheet, and enjoy checking on it yearly, you might have your bases covered.

Finding the Best Advisor

If 90% of advisors out there will give you the same service, how do you find the top 10% who will help you achieve your financial goals?

I put together this list of the **7 Questions You Absolutely Must Ask Your Advisor**[76] that will help you find one who will give you the best service out there while helping you align your investments with your values.

---

[76] Current or potential.

Adrian's Aside: Honesty Saves the Day

The financial industry has been serving itself for far too long, charging unnecessary fees to unknowing customers. There's a movement to help the industry clean up its act, but it's going to take brutal honesty.

In this chapter, I don't hold back. Yes, I'll get flack from old school advisors still riding high on commissions.

I hope it's obvious that I didn't hold back scrutiny on this list. The questions are invasive and to the point. But if you're going to hand over your financial future—and your values—to an advisor, you have the right to ask them every question on this list.

Thanks to this list of questions, many of you will end of breaking up with your advisor a*nd finding a better one. Don't worry, it's them, not you.*

7 Questions You Absolutely Must Ask Your Advisor

This is your cheat sheet. Take it into the meeting with your current or potential advisor. **Like your favorite class in school, this test is *Pass/Fail*.** If your advisor doesn't pass every question, it's time to say sayonara.

1. Are you a Registered Investment Advisor?

Registered Investment Advisor (RIA) is a certification, like MD[77] or CPA. RIAs have a "fiduciary" responsibility to you, their client. This is very important. Why? **Because "fiduciary" means they are legally obligated to put your interests first.** If an advisor is *not* an RIA, they do not have a legal obligation to put your interests first. This means they could sell you a scam and not get in trouble. Finding an advisor who is a fiduciary gives you extra protection and shows that the advisor is really looking out for your best interests to the best of their ability.

There are a select few Registered Investment Advisors out there. Of the 310,000 financial advisors in the U.S., about 10% of them are RIAs.

Answer to Pass: "Yes, I am a Registered Investment Advisor." Period.

---

[77] Hopefully your doctor has initials like this.

2. Is your firm affiliated with a broker-dealer?

You should be working with an advisor that is *not* affiliated with a broker-dealer[78].

Why? Some investment products like mutual funds, insurance, and annuities are commission-based, which means the person who *sells* you that investment gets a kick back. A big sales bonus could skew their judgement—they could be enticed to invest your money in a financial product that is not appropriate for you.

Fine print: While your advisor might have answered "yes" to Question 1 about being an RIA, if they answer "yes" to Question 2 about being affiliated with a broker-dealer, that means they could skip out on their fiduciary duty. Out of the 31,000 advisors that are RIAs, 26,000 of them are also registered with broker-dealers, meaning they could "switch hats" anytime they want to sell you something with commissions. Legally, this is a grey area that allows some RIAs to do something not in your best interest and still be protected under the law. Not fair, I know. But now you can sleuth out the truth.

In short, find an independent advisor that is *not* affiliated with a broker-dealer.

Answer to Pass: "No, I am *not* affiliated with a broker-dealer." Period.

3. Are you "fee-only"?

The fee-only model is a good model. Fee-only means the advisor gets paid either a flat fee or a percentage of the assets they manage for you. If an advisor gets paid "fee-only" they do *not* receive commissions from the investment products, like mutual funds, they sell.

Why is this important? The fee-only model helps reduce potential conflicts of interest.

---

[78] The term broker-dealer is used in U.S. securities regulation parlance to describe stock brokerages, because most of them act as both agents and principals. A brokerage acts as a broker (or agent) when it executes orders on behalf of clients, whereas it acts as a dealer, or principal, when it trades for its own account.

Fine print: If they say "fee-*based*" this could be a grey area, meaning they charge a fee *and* receive commissions.

To help find a "fee-only" advisor, you can start with the National Association of Personal Financial Advisors (NAPFA), the country's leading professional association of "fee-only" financial advisors.[79]

As a customer, you have right to know how your advisor gets paid. "Fee-only" is a good way to go.

Answer to Pass: "Yes, I get paid 'fee-*only*.'"

4. Do you or your firm receive third-party compensation for recommending certain investments?

This question is another way of asking Questions 2 and 3 and should finalize their compensation structure.

An advisor should *not* receive third-party compensation for recommending investments. Third-party compensation creates a conflict of interest, meaning they might not sell you something that's in your best interest.

Answer to Pass: "No, I do *not* receive third-party compensation for certain investments."

5. How you do approach asset allocation?

Asset allocation is explained in the Stock Marker primer in Part 3 of this book. If a professional advisor is worth the whistle they will have a *process* to help you determine an appropriate asset allocation for your investments.

They should at least ask you about:
- Goals
- Timeline
- Risk Tolerance

---

[79] NAPFA.org

A great advisor will get you know you and your family in hopes of building a lifetime customer. Their goal is to customize your asset allocation based on your real-time and future needs. They should also schedule yearly or biannual meetings to review your allocations and adjust them if anything has changed.

Answer to Pass: A detailed approach to asset allocation that includes goals, timeline, and risk tolerance.

6. Where will my money be held?

A proper fiduciary advisor will use a "third-party custodian"— like Fidelity, TD Ameritrade, or Schwab—to hold your funds.

You sign a limited power of attorney that gives the advisor the right to manage the money, but to *never* make withdrawals.

Answer to Pass: "Your money will be held with a third-party custodian (like Schwab or TD Ameritrade)."

7. How do you approach Sustainable Investing?

Many investment advisors still buy into the myth that sustainable investments are not good investments. This is understandable, since, until recently, advisors had limited options and were often misinformed.

Today, there is no excuse for an advisor to come up short when discussing a sustainable investing strategy. Truth be told, if they are not helping you find organizations and companies that aim to create long-term value through sustainable practices, they are mismanaging your money.

Advisors now have powerful tools at their disposal. For example, Morningstar, a ubiquitous investment research company, offers the Morningstar Sustainability Rating (used to rate the list of index funds and ETFs in the More Sustainable Stock Market chapter.) Advisors can easily look up the sustainability rating of over 20,000 funds.

Answer to Pass: An advisor should share an active understanding of sustainable investing, be up on the latest research, be open to your values, and willing to learn new things. If they say that sustainable investing is not profitable, they've been living in a cave. Go elsewhere.

These seven questions will help you land an advisor who is invested in your best interests.

How to Work With An Advisor

Just like any relationship, creating a winning sustainable investment strategy with your advisor will take work.

Set regular checkups | Meet at least once or twice per year, and check-in on performance, changes in your financial situation, and any upcoming financial needs.

Decipher risk and return | Many clients simply defer to their advisor when the advisor suggests investments that *outperform*. Many advisors are fixated on *maximizing* returns, meaning they want to make as much money as possible. This means they are also taking the most *risk* possible. **Instead of maximizing returns, advisors should be focused on *risk-adjusted returns*.** Risk-adjusted returns compare the level of risk two investments take. If investment A has a potential 12% return, but a high risk level, investment B with a 8% return and a low risk level might be a more appropriate investment for you. I'm a huge fan of risk-adjusted investments, like the YieldCos in the Renewable Energy chapter, whose stock price may not grow as much as Google's in a given year, yet they consistently pay out healthy dividends and have low risk of dropping in value.

Bring your ideas | Most advisors are focused on the stock market, which relegates them to large capital market investments. But perhaps you want to invest in affordable housing. They may make a fuss because it doesn't fit their system, but it's your money and you have the right to choose.

Advisors are skeptics—and for good reason. But instead of shooting down your ideas, they should help you research investments to understand the potential risks, rewards, and impacts.

Don't be afraid to approach your advisor with new ideas that you are excited about. Their job is to listen and explore the opportunity with you.

Top Sustainable Investment Advisors

After crunching answers to the *7 Questions You Absolutely Must Ask Your Advisor*, two investment advisory firms stand out. Both firms have a long-term commitment to sustainable investing and high standards when it comes to compensation.

Conscious Capital Management

Conscious Capital Management was founded by Brian Bengry after years of working with big banks like JP Morgan and Merrill Lynch. Brian witnessed the conflicting interests in high-pressure sales environments at old school firms. This approach hindered even the best advisors from providing conflict-free recommendations. He also saw the growing demand for socially responsible investments, so he set out to create a firm with the highest standards.

Conscious Capital Management is an example of a Registered Investment Advisor (RIA) with fiduciary responsibility. They are 100% independent and not affiliated with a broker-dealer. Their commitment to full transparency is evident as they list their fees on the website for everyone to see. Conscious Capital Management is focused solely on socially responsible investments.

Conscious Capital Management services:
- Simple Investing Services ($10,000 minimum)
- Personal Advisory Services ($250,000 minimum investment)
- Ethical Retirement Plans
- Financial Check-Ups

Conscious Capital Management's financial check-ups are like a casual visit to the doctor. They study your entire financial picture and work with you to create a holistic financial strategy. These reasonably-priced financial planning consultations are a great option for people who might not want continual advisory services, but can benefit from the insight of an expert.

Natural Investments

Natural Investments is one of the early movers of the socially responsible investing movement. They are a Registered Investment Advisor that works on a fee-only basis. They have 18 advisors across the U.S. and are committed to progressive values and communities.

Natural Investments can help high net worth investors place investments in community investing, organic agriculture, and forest conservation.

They are also active as shareholder advocates, meaning they write letters and lobby on behalf of their clients to create change. For example, they signed a letter to Wells Fargo and other banks urging them to avoid the risks associated with financing the Dakota Access Pipeline. They also signed a shareholder statement to a large agricultural company asking them to adopt zero-deforestation policies. **This type of action from an investment firm with hundreds of millions of dollars can create positive change.**

The minimum account size with Natural Investments is $50,000. They can also provide a comprehensive financial plan.

Other Advisors

As sustainable investing becomes a priority for *do-gooders* like you, top advisors around the world are shifting to keep up.

The following list is sourced by Toniic.com. It shows investment advisors around the world who are moving to 100% sustainable investing. To see the full spreadsheet, go to www.adrianreif.com/dogoodersguide .

Fine print: While these advisors aim for 100% sustainable investing, they may not all be Registered Investments Advisors from (See Question 1 above). Many of them also have high minimum investment amounts. For example, Abacus Wealth Partners charges a $2,400 yearly minimum fee. This will work for some of you, and not for others. You will need to determine which advisor is right for you.

Company Name	Advisor Name	Title	Location
Conscious Capital Management	Brian Bengry	Founder	Madison, WI
Natural Investments	Entire Firm		All 50 states
1919 Investment Counsel	Alison Bevilacqua	Principal	Cincinnati, OH USA
Abacus Wealth Partners	Brent Kessel	CEO	Santa Monica, CA USA
Align Impact, LLC	Jennifer Kenning	CEO	Santa Monica, CA USA
Ascent Private Capital Management	Jonathan Firestein	Managing Director	San Francisco, CA USA
Athena Capital Advisors	William McCalpin	Managing Partner	Lincoln, MA USA
Ballentine Partners, LLC	William Tickle	Director of Impact Investing	Boston, MA USA
Beyond Family Office	Orit Vaknin	Partner	Tel Aviv, Israel
Bienville Capital	Jack Meyercord	Head of Impact Investments	Boston, MA USA
Blended Value Group	Jed Emerson	Founder	San Francisco, CA USA
Bridges Ventures	Clara Barby	Partner and Head of Impact+	London, UK
Brownson, Rehmus & Foxworth	Adam Durfee	Lead Advisor	San Francisco, CA
Cambridge Associates	Jessica Matthews	Managing Director	San Francisco, CA USA
Challenger 88	Wolfgang Hafenmayer	Partner	Zurich, Switzerland
Colorado Capital Management, Inc.	Steven Ellis	President	Denver, CO USA

Adrian Reif

First Affirmative Financial Network	Laura Isanuk	Business Manager	Denver, CO USA
Future-Fit Foundation	Martin Rich	Co-founder	London, UK
Grieg Investor	Gudleik Njå	Partner	Oslo, Norway
HIP (Human Impact + Profit) Investor Inc	R. Paul Herman	CEO	San Francisco, CA USA
I-DEV International	Patricia Chin-Sweeney	Senior Partner	San Francisco, CA USA
IVM Caring Capital	Hans Volberda	Partner	Amsterdam, Netherlands
Merrill Lynch	Harrison Fischer	Financial Advisor	New York, NY USA
Merrill Lynch	Mary Foust Alena Meeker	Senior Vice President	San Francisco, CA USA
MissionPoint Partners	Adam Rein	Managing Director	Boston, MA USA
Morgan Stanley	Dan Rosenstein	Financial Advisor	New York, NY San Francisco, CA USA
onValues Ltd.	Ivo Knoepfel	Founder and Director	Zurich, Switzerland
Open Capital Advisors	Annie Roberts	Partner	Nairobi, Kenya
Principium Investments, LLC	Michael Tracy, CFP	Chief Investment Officer	Boulder, CO USA
Roots of Impact	Bjoern Struewer	Founder & CEO	Frankfurt, Germany
Snowball LLP	Paul Blyth	Investment Director	London, UK
SNW Asset Management	Glen Yelton	Head of Impact Investing	Johnson City, TN USA
Sonen Capital	Raúl Pomares	Founder	San Francisco, CA USA

180

UBS Financial Services	Kathy Leonard	Senior Vice President	Denver, CO USA
Unitus Capital	Neha Mudaliar	Director	Bangalore, India
Veris Wealth Partners	Casey Verbeck	Director	Boulder, CO USA
Wire Group	Tera Terpstra	Managing Partner	Utrecht, Netherlands

Investment Advisor—Review

Investment advisors are coaches who can help you get your investing game on track. But not all advisors are created equal.

- Advisors can get paid in three ways. Opt for "fee-only" or financial planning consultations over commission-based advisors, which creates a conflict of interest.
- If hiring an advisor will help you sleep better or get your financial life in shape, it's likely a good investment.
- Ask your current or potential advisor the *7 Absolute Must-Ask Questions* below.
- Conscious Capital Management and Natural Investments are two independent firms that solely manage sustainable investments for people like you.
- It's your money—you deserve an advisor who is going to treat it with the respect you do.
- Go to www.adrianreif.com/dogoodersguide to see a list of advisors around the world working towards advising 100% sustainable portfolios.

The 7 Absolute Must-Ask Questions	
Question:	**Answer to Pass:**
1. Are you a Registered Investment Advisor?	Yes. Period.
2. Is your firm affiliated with a broker-dealer?	No. Period.
3. Are you "fee-only"?	Yes.
4. Do you or your firm receive third-party compensation for recommending certain investments?	No.
5. How you do approach asset allocation?	A detailed approach to asset allocation that includes goals, timeline, and risk tolerance.
6. Where will my money be held?	With a third-party custodian.
7. How do you approach Sustainable Investing?	Already have sustainable investing knowledge, be interested in your values, and be willing to learn new things. If they think sustainable investing is not profitable, they haven't looked at the research.

Bonus Chapter: Greening Your Home as an Investment

A few years ago, I found myself standing on a steeply-pitched and dilapidated roof, with a $5 rope from Home Depot securing my harness to a equally dilapidated chimney. Best case scenario, I fall off and the $5 rope keeps me from hitting the ground with an abrupt, potentially backbreaking, jolt. I didn't ponder the worst case.

I don't recommend this. But I do recommend getting intimate with your roof. In this case, I was helping a friend haul solar panels onto his roof. We installed several panels six months before and they were producing so much renewable energy that he decided to squeeze more onto the remaining space of empty, yet valuable shingles.

Solar panels are great investments, but your home is full of overlooked sustainable investing opportunities that can deliver big returns.

This is not where I tell you to drop your thermostat to 65 degrees in the winter and raise it to 78 in the summer. If you like wearing three layers all winter, I'm all for it. But I believe our sustainable advances can be comfortable, profitable, and sustainable, especially if we're counting on everyone to join in. When I built my family's new house in 2017, I spent countless hours finding the most sustainable—and simple and comfortable—strategies and investments for making our house a net-zero user of energy.

In this bonus chapter, I am going to show you how to make money in the form of energy savings by investing in the sustainability of your home.

Why Better Buildings

Buildings, including our homes, account for 39% of U.S. greenhouse gas emissions. This is more than the transportation and industrial sectors.

Buildings also consume 70% of the electricity load in the U.S. Given that 64% of U.S. energy comes from coal and nuclear power, every time you open the refrigerator door or make tea is like clinking a pick axe into the side of a mountain—and one of the biggest sources CO_2 emissions.

The green building industry is booming as developers, building owners, and occupants recognize the serious repercussions to the footprint—and the huge cost savings that come with green building.

The proof is in the green pudding. Green buildings pay for themselves quickly. For example, energy-efficient buildings that are LEED-Certified have 34% lower CO_2 emissions and consume 25% less energy.[80] Saving energy is saving money.

Most green building techniques are accomplished with simple investments in energy efficiency and a few new technologies that pay for themselves quickly while keeping you comfortable. They also offer shockingly profitable investment returns.

An Eco-Friendly Capitalist—With Chaps

Meet Dave. Dave is a close friend who inspired this chapter. If you ever meet him on Halloween, you'll know he's a fun loving guy. Especially if he's wearing his famous chaps.

Dave's a capitalist who invests with savvy, owns a few rental houses, and is known to bring friends together around a meal or campfire. A guitar eventually makes its way into his hands and everyone is invited to sing along.

After scooping up a *vintage* 90-year old, three-story foreclosure several years ago, Dave hosted a good ol' fashion "clean out my foreclosed house" party. But the "help put solar panels on my house" party was even better.

A few years later, I asked Dave about how his solar panels were doing. He sent me a spreadsheet and we began to talk about the impressive ROI, not just the latest inverters on the market.[81] It turns out solar panels can generate a healthy investment return. I soon wondered what other sustainable home improvements could also generate profitable returns.

In the pages ahead, you'll find twelve different home improvements and their potential financial returns.

---

[80] LEED stands for Leadership in Energy and Environmental Design.
[81] Do check out SolarEdge's power optimizers.

Adrian's Aside: Clean Energy Hack

One of my favorite clean energy hacks is as easy as a few clicks. No dangling from questionable ropes on questionable roofs tied off to questionable chimneys.

Arcadia Power allows you to link your utilities account to 100% renewable energy from wind power. All you have to do is create an account, enter your utility information, and Arcadia Power will start powering your home or apartment with clean energy.

Better yet, you can switch to 50% clean electricity *for free*. If you switch to 100% wind power, it adds about $5-$15 per month to your electricity bill. Go to www.adrianreif.com/dogoodersguide to get $25 off your next electricity bill.

Profitable Home Investments

Energy is a building's largest environmental footprint and ongoing cost.

Just like investing in the stock market, these investments can provide real returns, while directly lowering your home's footprint.

Energy Efficiency Investment	Estimated Return
Energy audit	n/a
LED light bulbs	750%
Improved insulation	15%
Energy-efficient hot water heater	6.70%
Energy Star windows	100%
Solar panels	4%-28%
Mini-split A/C	5%-20%
Power Sensor	9%
Water Efficiency Investment	Estimated Return
High-efficiency shower head	10%
Ultra-high efficiency toilet	3%
Drip irrigation	varies
Greywater system	0%, but still really cool

Energy Audit

An energy audit assesses your home's energy use and inefficiencies. A professional energy auditor can give your home a checkup. They will check for things like leaks, insulation, inspect ductwork, and use infrared cameras to see where the home could be losing heat. A home energy audit costs between $200 – $600 and could identify the most investable ways to save money with your home.

LED Lights

LED lights are serious money makers. They use at least 75% less energy and last 25 times longer than regular light bulbs (and outperform CFLs, too). LED lights have dropped in price. You can find them for $4 each online and in stores.

The return on investment for LEDs is 750% and pays itself back in two months. **This beats every investment in this book.**

Potential return: If you replaced 30 standard bulbs with LEDs, you'd save $9,000 over the next 10 years. LEDs pay themselves back in two months and have a 750% return on investment.

Improved Insulation

Boosting an attic's insulation from R-11 (the measure of insulation value) to R-49 should cost $1,500 for materials and labor and save you $600 per year on heating costs.[82]

Potential return: Insulating an attic could return 40% in year one alone. You could save an additional $6,000 over the next 10 years, for an annualized return on investment of 15%.

---

[82] An energy audit will show you where your home could use more insulation.

Energy Efficient Hot Water Heater

Heating water accounts for about *15% of a home's energy use*. High efficiency water heaters use between 10% and 60% less energy than standard models.[83]

I recommend an on-demand (tankless) water heater, which saves energy by heating water "on-demand,"or as it is needed, instead of storing it in a big tank and keeping it hot. Tankless water heaters save 45-60% of the energy compared to typical water heaters. I personally love them. My home uses a Stiebel Eltron on-demand hot water heater for *all* its hot water needs.

A tankless water heater costs between $500 and $1,200 depending on the size and quality, plus about $1,000 for installation. For this calculation, let's assume a $900 water heater and $1,000 for installation.

Potential Return: In this example, a new tankless water heater should save you about $370/year. Over 22 years (the life of the water heater), you will save $8,000, which is a yearly return of 6.7%.

Window Upgrades

A simple Energy Star rated window—which are very common—will save you $257/year when replacing old, single pane windows. This will pay for itself within the year.

Potential return: Over ten years, a single window could save you $2,570, with an annualized return on investment of 99%.

Solar Panels

Solar panels allow your roof or side yard (i.e. pole mounted panels) to manufacture reliable, renewable electricity.

The return on solar panels is highly state dependent and relies on the amount of rebates, electricity costs, and net metering. Some states, like

---

[83] EnergyStar.gov

Mississippi have backward policies that make it hard to invest in producing *your own* electricity.

For example, in Massachusetts a 5-kilowatt solar panel system pays for itself in 4 years and earns you 28% per year. After that, your energy is free until the panels need to be replaced!

In Mississippi, a 5-kilowatt solar panel system pays for itself in 16 years and earns you 4.6% a year—still not a bad return for clean energy!

Top states for solar are Massachusetts, New Jersey, Rhode Island, Oregon, New York, Maryland, Connecticut, Vermont, DC, New Hampshire, Minnesota, Colorado, Delaware, New Mexico, Hawaii and California.[84]

Potential Return: A 5kw solar panel system in Massachusetts and other solar-friendly states can earn a 28% return on investment, better than most investments in this book.

Mini-Split Heat Pump and A/C

Heating and cooling your home is responsible for about 50% of your home's energy use (up to 66% in colder states).

Mini-split heat pumps heat and cool your home for a fraction of the cost of standard air conditioners and forced air heating systems.

Mini-splits are popular in Asia, but have taken a while to catch on the U.S. But mini-splits are catching on thanks to the inefficiency of standard ductwork (the big silver rectangle things), which lose about 30% of the energy created to heat or cool air in your house.

If the average home invested in a ductless mini-split, the owners would save about $560 per year, or $11,200 over the 20-year life of the unit.

Potential Return: An investment of $4,500 in mini-splits for heating and cooling your home would return 4.6% per year (without factoring in the cost of a new HVAC system. If you chose a mini-split over a new HVAC system, the investment would return 20% per year).

---

[84] Go to the website SolarPowerRocks.com and choose "state rankings" to help you estimate returns for solar power in your state.

Home Energy Sensor

When I built my house, I installed a Sense Energy Monitor in my home. The monitor clips in to the electric panel and provides a detailed readout of the house's energy use via the Sense App. The App allows you to see what percentage of electricity is used by each device, or how small things like leaving the bathroom fan on all day can add up. Armed with this information, you can make wiser decisions about your behavior, or detect anomalies, say a refrigerator running longer than normal.

Potential Return: Assuming a home energy monitor like Sense (which costs only $250) can save you 5% on your electricity use each year for the next 20 years, a $250 investment returns 9% per year.

Pro Tip: Rebates and Tax Credits

The previous calculations were made *without* factoring in potential rebates and tax credits. Every state has a list of rebates and tax credits for energy efficiency and renewable energy improvements. You can find a list of incentives for each state at Database of State Incentives for Renewables & Efficiency website, DSIREUSA.org.

For example, Colorado offers rebates when you buy Energy Star appliances, get an energy audit, or add attic insulation.

Example rebates in Colorado (and many other states):
*Attic Insulation: 30% of cost
Air Sealing/Weather-Stripping: 30% of cost
*High Efficiency Lighting: 30% of cost
*Wall Insulation: $800
Evaporative Cooling System: $200 - $1200
Central Air Conditioner (New): $400 - $700
Central Air Conditioner (Trade In): $550
Ground Source/Geothermal Heat Pump: $300 per ton
Electric Heat Pump: $450
Programmable Thermostat: $25
High Efficiency Furnace: $400

Electrically Commuted Motor (for furnace fan): $200
*Tankless Water Heater: $100
Standard Tank Water Heater: $70
ENERGY STAR Refrigerator: $15
ENERGY STAR Dishwasher: $10
ENERGY STAR Clothes Washer: $50

When you add the savings from rebates for energy efficiency your investment returns grow.

Water Use

Water costs tend to be overlooked because water is cheap, but with drought conditions worsening and underground aquifers drying up, it's time to think harder about making a splash in our water footprint. Consider that the average person uses 60 to 100 gallons of household water per day.

Most do-gooders are already water conscious, but these hacks can help you save even more water while earning money.

High-Efficiency Shower Head

The best shower head on the market is the Tri-Max Showerhead by Niagara Conservation. You can choose from three settings: 0.5 / 1 / 1.5 gallons per minute. It costs $10.

Potential Return: If you switched from a 2 gallons per minute shower head to a Tri-Max (at an average of 0.75 GPM), you would save 5 gallons per shower (5 minute shower). That means 18,250 gallons saved over 10 years and an annual return on investment of 10%.

Ultra-High Efficiency Toilet

When I built my house I scoured high and low for *the best* toilet on the market. A throne for a king, you might say. I found it with Niagara Conservation, who reinvented the toilet with the Stealth.

The Stealth is not your typical rinky-dinky low-flow toilet. The redesigned flush chamber uses vacuum pressure to flush powerfully, yet quietly. You can choose from two flush settings: 0.5 and 0.95 gallons per flush (GPF), making it *by far* the lowest water use toilet on the market.

Potential Return: The average home flushes the toilet 5 times per day. Over ten years, your toilet will cost you about $300 in water costs. If you buy a Niagara Stealth toilet over a standard 1.6 GPF toilet, you'll save $160 in water costs, (and 14,000 gallons of water) which returns you about 3% per year. The Stealth is an even bigger winner for high-volume locations like hotels, offices, and airports.

Drip Irrigation

If your landscape needs water you can lower your water footprint and save money by switching to a drip irrigation system. P.S. *If you're still watering a massive patch of grass, we might need to talk.*

A drip irrigation system is a low-pressure and low-water delivery system for landscaping and gardening that helps you pinpoint trees and plants.

You can run drip irrigation lines under mulch and even attach an inexpensive timer to the faucet that will turn it on and off daily, depending on the season. Drip irrigation saves water from evaporating and keeps roots moist without overly soaking them. Check out your local hardware store to get setup.

Potential return: Drip irrigation's return on investment varies dramatically based on how much you water and where you live.

Greywater System

"Grey water" is *used* water, typically from your shower and washing machine. This water can be used again to water your landscaping. Note: Phosphate-free detergents and biodegradable soaps are best.

My greywater system—designed with the help of a greywater consultant—is designed to transport used shower and washing machine water out the back of the house, reusing the water to water landscape. For DIY tips, visit Greywater Action's website and go from there.

Potential Return: After crunching the numbers, the investment in extra plumbing, a diverter, and pump does not return a positive investment. *But the cool factor is still positive!*

Green Home Investments—Review

Investing in your home's energy and water footprint can generate serious financial returns while lightening your energy footprint.

- Buildings generate 39% of the U.S. greenhouse gas emissions.
- Green, LEED-certified building use 25% less energy, have 34% lower CO2 emissions, and pay for themselves quickly.
- Your home is full of overlooked money-making opportunities.
- State rebates can boost your savings even more (search DSIRE).

Energy Efficiency Investment	Estimated Return
Energy audit	n/a
LED light bulbs	750%
Improved insulation	15%
Energy-efficient hot water heater	6.70%
Energy Star windows	100%
Solar panels	4%-28%
Mini-split A/C	5%-20%
Power Sensor	9%
Water Efficiency Investment	Estimated Return
High-efficiency shower head	10%
Ultra-high efficiency toilet	3%
Drip irrigation	varies
Greywater system	0%, but still really cool

The Changing Landscape

So there you have it—hundreds of world-changing investments at your fingertips.

Because the sustainable investing landscape can evolve rapidly, I created a free email club that reports on changes in sustainable investing for everyday investors.

We keep you up-to-date with straight-to-your-inbox updates like:

- New investment launches
- Updates to existing investments
- Asset allocation research
- Interviews and advice from other experts

To stay ahead of the sustainable investing curve, go to:
www.adrianreif.com/dogoodersguide

"EVERYTHING AROUND
YOU THAT YOU CALL
LIFE WAS MADE UP BY
PEOPLE THAT WERE NO
SMARTER THAN YOU
AND YOU CAN CHANGE
IT. YOU CAN INFLUENCE
IT. YOU CAN BUILD
YOUR OWN THINGS
THAT OTHER PEOPLE
CAN USE.

ONCE YOU LEARN THAT,
YOU'LL NEVER BE THE
SAME AGAIN."

—STEVE JOBS

PART 3

BUILDING YOUR PORTFOLIO

Part 3 Introduction

But first, congrats. Part 2 was a lot. If your head feels like a mosquito gorging at a backyard BBQ, just bathe in the epicurean bliss.

Part 2 is designed to prime your brain—like spreading all the puzzle pieces face up on the table before snapping them into place.

In the pages ahead, we'll turn the puzzle pieces into a world-class portfolio built just for you.

Investing Primer

If you need a jumpstart on the core principles of successful investing, the next 22 pages contain an *investing primer* designed to quickly explain the core ideas that lay the basis for successful investing. Part of my mission is to help you become a better investor so that you can grow your money while making a difference.

In this primer, you'll learn:
1. Three Secrets of Investing
2. Why & How to Avoid Killer Fees
3. How to Find Your Asset Allocation, and more.

If you are *already well-versed* in these matters, you can skip ahead to Designing a World-Class Portfolio.

Onward.

Investing Primer

Projects are due. Kids need to be picked up. Your sweetie needs some lovin'.[85] Is your life *busy*, or *rich*?

In a world where we have the luxury of being "busy," we often forget how rich life can be. When our lives are "busy" we don't have time to invest in the lives we really want—financial abundance, community that fulfills us, and purposeful work. But when we lead rich lives, investing in growth is something we savor.

So I have to ask: Do you *really* want the life you want? A life rich with financial abundance, fulfilling community, and meaning and purpose?

I ask because many people expect financial abundance, fulfilling community, and purposeful work to just show up. They want the "5 Tips" article they cram into their walk to the subway. They don't want to put in the time, but they want the best results.

Investing Wisely

I'm not a finance guru, but I do know that when you invest in your financial health, you will reap the rewards. The good news is that investing is *not* reserved for "the finance guy." Everybody can invest wisely.

Successful investing is built on a few fundamental laws. Once you get those, you're set for life. But understanding and implementing these fundamental laws takes effort.

Investing Primer

There are things schools do not teach us that are essential for life. If you didn't have someone to teach you investing, odds are you're scared to death of it. In order to prep you for Part 3—Designing a World-Class Portfolio—this chapter is designed to get you up to speed on the fundamental rules of investing.

---

[85] Like, hugs and stuff, you fiend!

Secrets of Investing

Michael Pollan's *In Defense of Food* simplified healthy eating for a lot of people—"Eat real food. Not too much. Mostly plants."

I'll offer my investing rules—**"Start early. Diversify like a pro. Avoid fees."**

These secrets were once reserved for "finance people," but once you master them you'll be on your way to financial wealth.[86]

Investing Secret #1 — Start Early

Like a finely crafted Japanese blade, compounding is simple, yet powerful. Some have even called it the *8th Wonder of the World*. Current legend ascribes to Einstein the meme that *compound interest is the greatest human invention*.[87] Nearly every book on investing or money management pays homage to *compounding*, so I'll spend only a minute here.

Compounding allows your money to grow on itself, like a cartoon snowball rolling down a hill. The snowball starts small, but as it rolls down the hill it picks up more snow. As the surface area increases, it picks up even more snow! The earlier you start to invest, the more time there is for compounding to work its magic.

Let's talk real money. If your $100,000 investment account earns 10% in a year, it's now worth $110,000. If the new $110,000 stays invested and earns 10% the next year, it doesn't just earn another $10k. It earns $11,000. Add that to your $110k and you've got $121k. Over 20 years, that $100K compounds to $673,000.

The real power of compounding shows up in this example in the last year. From Year 19 to 20, your money earns $61,159 in the final year thanks to compounding interest.

The example above is a simple one, with the same interest rate earned every year. In reality, your investments will grow variable amounts every year. On average, the stock market grows 7.7% per year, but some years it goes up 20%, other years it goes down 20%. The down years have a

---

[86] I promise riches *if* you promise to follow these rules and wait 30 years.
[87] There's little evidence to prove Einstein said this, but it makes for a great point, eh?

disproportionate impact on compounding. For example, if you lose 20% of your portfolio's value this year, you have to earn 25% the next year just to get back to where you started. This is why Warren Buffet's No. 1 Rule of Investing is "Don't lose money." In the sections ahead, we'll discuss how diversifying like a pro can help you *not lose money*.

In short: The best day to start investing was 20 years ago. If you didn't start then, the next best day is today.

Because this book's gift to the world is not the intricacies of compounding, let's move on.

Investing Secret #2 — Diversify Like a Pro

When the Kentucky Derby rolled around last May, did you take the money in your 401k and bet it on the horse sporting your favorite colors?! Of course not! You bet it on the one with the coolest name. Go *Spend A Buck*![88]

Betting on one horse is exciting, but it's no way to invest for the long-term. Diversification is a long-term investing strategy that can help you make it through down markets, while growing your money.

If you take one thing away from this book, let it be this: **Diversification helps you manage risk.** And it's *not* as hard as you think.

Another term for diversification is *asset allocation*. Yep, we just got fancy, but if you're going to diversify like a pro, you can talk like a pro, too.

"Asset allocation" refers to how we allocate our assets—or how wisely you diversify them. "Assets" are the things you own. Cash, savings accounts, stocks, bonds, real estate, beanie babies. "Allocation" is how those assets are allocated—what percent is in stocks, bonds, savings, real estate, etc.

You can use asset allocation strategies to help you accomplish your particular goals—like saving for college, or planning for retirement—because the strategies have been used for long periods of time and tend to perform in certain ways based on historical performance. In Part 3, we discuss *all-weather* allocations, which are the most recent take on ideal

---

[88] I only know this name because this horse won the year I was born. My parents assume it's why I'm prone to spending so much money.

portfolio diversifications that grow in good times, but don't lose money in bad times.

To really understand diversification, we need to talk about Easter. This Easter you managed to outsmart your five-year-old niece and found all of the hidden plastic eggs before she did.[89] Your pink plastic basket is overflowing with riches. The smell of pungent iron and copper tickle your nose. It's yours! All yours!

Until a giant eagle descends on you—its glare ice cold as it calmly plucks the pink basket from your sweaty hands. (Hey, at least you didn't freak out.)

You've heard the cliché: *Don't put all of your eggs in one basket!* I'm mostly sure this is where that phrase originated. But how do we protect our money from greedy eagles?

It turns out, asset allocation is the number one factor that explains the returns for an investment portfolio—whether it lost money, gained a little money, or gained a lot. It can help us protect our assets from a random eagle attack.

Let's take a deeper look at asset allocation and how to diversify like a pro, then we can see how we could have protected your eggs from the giant eagle. In Part 3, we'll look at world-class asset allocations used by billionaire investors who've turned $1 billion into $23 billion.

The Ins and Outs of Asset Allocation

From 2005-2010 the fine folks of Generation X lost 55% of their median net worth.[xv] How did this happen? A large portion of their money was invested in the stock market. When the stock market took a nosedive, so did their money. However, not every portfolio will react like this, so it's important you choose an asset allocation strategy for your portfolio that meets your needs.

The chart below shows four common asset allocation strategies for an investment portfolio including their performance from 1926 to 2016.

---

[89] So what, I'm competitive. Don't judge.

	Conservative	Balanced	Growth	Aggressive growth
U.S. stock / Foreign stock / Bond / Short-term investments	6% / 14% / 30% / 50%	10% / 15% / 35% / 40%	5% / 21% / 49% / 25%	25% / 60% / 15%
Annual return %				
Average	5.96	7.91	8.88	9.55
Worst one-year return	–17.67	–40.64	–52.92	–60.78
Best one-year return	31.06	76.57	109.55	136.07
Worst 20-year return	2.92	3.43	3.10	2.66
Best 20-year return	10.98	13.83	15.34	16.49
Historical volatility	4.52	9.61	13.13	15.83

The "Conservative" allocation (which does not refer to Republican investors) shows the lowest amount of historical volatility, or amount the portfolio fluctuated up and down. You can also see this reflected in the worst one-year return of -17.67%, which is lower than all other portfolios.

Asset Classes

If you compare the portfolios above, you'll notice they have different average returns, worst one-year returns, volatility, etc. This is because each portfolio has a different asset allocation—different percentages allocated to different asset classes:

- U.S. stock
- Foreign stock
- Bonds
- Short-term investments (CDs, savings accounts, etc.)

These are four common asset classes, but don't include others like commodities, gold, real estate, or fixed-return, like several of the investments mentioned earlier in this book.

Each of these asset classes perform differently in different economic "seasons." For example, when economic growth is good, stocks do well and bonds will underperform stocks. When economic growth is slowing, historical data shows investors move their money to less-risky bonds, and bonds will tend to perform better during that season. You'll also notice the portfolios have tradeoffs—the lower the risk, the lower the average returns.

Risk-Return Tradeoff

Each asset class can be classified on the risk—return spectrum based on historical performance. "Risk" means the likelihood of it failing, i.e. losing your money. "Return" means the amount of money generated by an investment.

Chart: Risk-Return Tradeoff

The asset classes mentioned above are expected to perform as follows:
- Foreign stocks—Highest risk, highest potential return.
- U.S. stock—Moderate risk, moderate potential return.
- Bonds —Very little risk, consistent, but small return.
- Short-term investments—Almost no risk, very small return.

Like most things in life, the higher risk you take, the higher the *potential* reward. Gambling is a great example of high risk / high potential reward.

Black Jack could pay off big, but most of the time you go home with less money than you started with. Savings accounts offer virtually zero risk—they are guaranteed by the FDIC insurance—and offer small rewards.

Some things are medium risk, medium reward, like eating a cheeseburger. Will you die of a heart attack *right away*? Meh, not likely. Will it be tasty? Most likely.

But not everyone has the same risk-reward appetite. That same cheeseburger for people like me who are "ungifted in the lactose arts" is a high immediate risk to my intestines (and overall happiness). The tasty reward isn't worth it.

Here's how typical investments stack up along the risk-reward spectrum.

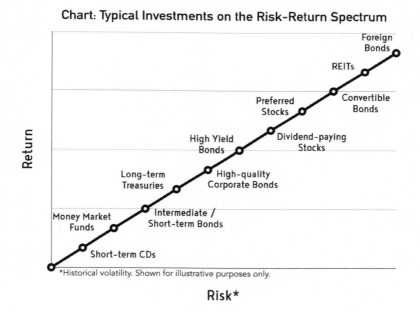

Chart: Typical Investments on the Risk-Return Spectrum

Risk and Easter Baskets

Back to Easter baskets. You could keep all of your Easter eggs in your favorite shiny pink plastic basket, but now you know they are at risk should a giant eagle be in the area.

Diversification can help you decide which baskets to put those eggs in to make sure you have enough for when you need them, but not at 100% risk. You could put some in a steel, fireproof basket in the basement, locked down for emergencies. You could put some eggs in a nice wicker basket and leave it in on the front porch, where your friends can stop by and fill it up with even more goodies (or a neighbor could get greedy and take everything). You could put some in a beautiful picnic basket nestled in the crook of your arm, ready to use but not fully exposed to risk.

Asset Allocation and Underwear

Your asset allocation should fit you just like your favorite pair of underwear. And, yes, you'll want to change it every so often.

Asset allocation depends on these key considerations:

Goals	What are you trying to do with the money? Grow it? Preserve it?
Risk Tolerance	How much risk can you handle?
Timeline	When do you need the money?

Goals

It is important to have a goal when you decide how your money is invested.
- Are you investing for retirement? This means, the money is essential to your way of life once you retire.
- Are you aiming to grow the money as much as possible?
- Are you going to use the money as a down payment for a house?
- Are you going to use it to start a business?
- Are you saving it for scuba diving in Micronesia next year?

Risk Tolerance

Ask yourself: "How willing am I to lose this money?" "How do I respond watching my money go up and down?"

After talking with dozens of other investors—and investing my own money for the last 16 years—I've found that most of us are *not* as risk tolerant as we think we are.

Try this: Imagine putting $500,000 of your hard-earned money into an account. Now, imagine signing in to your account for your monthly check in and you see the money has dropped in value to $450,000. When you sign in next month, the money is worth $400,000. Now $350,000. Now $300,000. Personally, I'm feeling a little nauseous just writing this. How about you? Unless you've mastered Pema Chödrön's latest techniques, your tummy is probably fluttering.

Risk is real—don't let it be an abstract thought exercise. In 2008, I watched as a close friend's $1,000,000 nest egg wilted to $500,000. I don't recommend you wait for real life to help you find your risk tolerance.

Pro tip: If you want to better understand your risk tolerance, search "Edward Jones risk tolerance questionnaire." The free survey will give you a good idea of what your current risk tolerance is for your investments. A good advisor should also be able to help you feel into your actual risk tolerance based on your past behaviors. Did you actually ride out the 38% losses of the Great Recession or did you sell everything to stop panicking?

As a reminder, your risk tolerance is personal to you. Don't be lured by the *shoulds* of standardized investing advice.

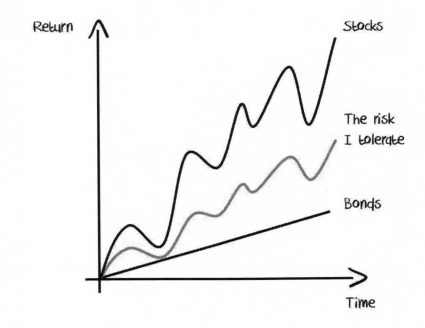

Timeline

The third factor that helps determine asset allocation is the amount of time you are investing for. Investments fluctuate, especially stocks. Imagine it is 2008 again, and you're planning to retire in 2009. If your retirement money was invested heavily in stocks and lost 38% of its value, you might have to work another several years. But if you were early in life and you wouldn't need the money for another 30 years, you could have weathered the big drop.

The conventional approach to timeline is to move your asset allocation from *aggressive-growth* in earlier years to *conservative* in later years. Stocks are considered aggressive growth and bonds, or cash for the really risk averse, are considered the most conservative.

Keep in mind, this is the *conventional* approach and is generally good advice. However, as you gain more confidence in your investing experience, you'll begin to see that the linear relationships presented above—"I don't like risk therefore my money won't grow as much"—are not always true.

Engagement

In addition to goals, risk tolerance, and timeline, a fourth factor that determines how to invest is your *desire*. How engaged are you and do you want to be? Do you enjoy researching the holdings in an ETF, or do you want to set-it-and-forget-it? Do you want to pull out your spreadsheet and rebalance your portfolio twice a year or do you want your advisor or robo-advisor to do it for you?

Rebalancing

Back to underwear for a second. Apparently it's a good idea to buy new underwear every 12 to 18 months.[90] This is a good time to rebalance your portfolio, too.

Rebalancing is a key tool to diversifying like a pro. It keeps your portfolio inline with its target allocation percentages over time.

Let's say you have a "balanced" portfolio that targets owning 35% U.S. stocks. If over the last 12 to 18 months those stocks have grown significantly in

---

[90] Yes, this was an epiphany for me, too.

value, they will be more than 35% of your portfolio. Human nature might tease you into keeping the money in those stocks, since they've done well. Just like you are tempted to keep that underwear because they "haven't fallen apart yet."

Let's say the stocks are now 45% of your total portfolio (because they've grown in value). Your portfolio is facing more risk than its optimal target. It's time to sell some of your stocks to bring the percentage back to 35%. By the way, this works the other way, too. If stocks dip, you'll want to sell other investments and use the money to buy more stocks, likely getting them at discount prices.

When to Rebalance

If you rebalance too often, say every month, the cost of transaction fees for buying and selling may cost you more money than its worth. The general advice is to rebalance every 12 to 18 months.

But you may need to rebalance at other times, too. If a certain asset class has a hot run over the last 3 months and brings your allocation out of alignment, this is a sign you may need to rebalance.

Life events can also trigger a need to rebalance. Did you get a new, high-paying job and want to take more risk with the extra cash? Did you lose a job and need to reduce your risk? Is retirement getting closer?

Rebalancing will ultimately lead to a healthier and more successful portfolio and is worth the effort. If you don't want to do it, find an advisor who can help.

What's the Best Asset Allocation for You?

After all this talk of diversifying like a pro and asset allocation, you probably just want to know what the best asset allocation is for you, right? I knew you were going to ask. And *you* knew I was going to say, "It depends."[91]

I'd be doing you a disservice if I pointed you to one asset allocation. Later in Part 3, you'll see four real world do-gooder portfolios from four really smart investors and none of them are the same. But, I will help you design a portfolio based on your needs in the chapters ahead.

In general, there are two ways to begin understanding which asset allocation will work for you:

---

[91] I feel like we're really clicking!

1. Use IPERS Asset Allocation Calculator
2. Study Vanguard Target Retirement Funds

IPERS Asset Allocation Calculator

The Iowa Public Employees' Retirement System (IPERS) website hosts a basic asset allocation calculator with recommendations based on your age, current assets, risk tolerance, and more.[92]

If you run the IPERS calculator for a person who is 45 years old, has current assets of $500,000, plans to save $10,000 per year, and has a "balanced" risk tolerance, the calculator suggests a portfolio of:

- 72% stocks
- 16% bonds
- 12% cash

One drawback to this allocation is the very high allocation to stocks, which will cause it to drop during another recession. It also leaves out asset classes like real estate, U.S. treasury bills, and foreign markets, all of which could help the portfolio perform during differing economic seasons.

Vanguard Target Retirement Funds

Many 401Ks and financial gurus will offer you off-the-shelf "retirement funds." These funds rebalance themselves every so often as you move closer to retirement.

If you borrowed the asset allocation from the Vanguard Target Retirement 2055 Fund, which is designed for someone who plans to retire between 2053 and 2057, the recommended asset allocation would be:

- 54% U.S. Stocks
- 36% International Stocks
- 7% Bonds
- 3% International Bonds

I don't like these Target Retirement funds for several reasons. One, they give everyone the same allocation based on age. We've already learned this is not personalized to you. Two, they generally carry higher fees, eating

---

[92] Search "IPERS Asset Allocation"

into your returns. Three, they are very high-risk, with 90% allocation to stocks, and leave out other asset classes like IPERS does.

There are two situations where these funds may be appropriate. If you are a 100% hands-off investor and truly want to set-it-and-forget-it, this could be for you. Second, if you're a high-income earner and have no concerns that you'll meet your retirement needs, this is a fine way to make your investing more convenient. If the fund doesn't perform well, you won't be impacted.

Investing Secret #3 – Avoid Fees

Now that you're in on the first two secrets of investing—start early, diversify like a pro—it's time to learn something that very few people know. I say this because despite a 16-year investing history, I didn't really understand it until I dove in deep for this book.

Fees are one of the most insidious drains on your investing gains—and your retirement account or advisor is willingly charging you.

Beware the Killer Fees

Enter Jack Bogle.

Jack is the founder of Vanguard, an investment company with over $3 trillion—like trillion with a T—under management. I happen to like Jack. He's been on a crusade to help everyday investors level the playing field when it comes to the fees charged by their financial products.

According to Jack, "If you made a one-time investment of $10,000 at age twenty, and, assuming, 7% annual growth over time, you would have $574,464 by the time you're nearly eighty.

"But, if you paid 2.5% in total management fees and other expenses, your ending account balance would only be $140,274 over the same period."[xvi]

$574,000 or $140,000? I'll let you choose.[93]

---

[93] If you are wondering how this happens, the 2.5% in fees reduce the earnings each year. Thus, there is less money to benefit from the power of compounding. 2.5% seems small to us, but it's huge over time.

Just What Fees Are We Talking About?

Mutual funds have fees on fees on fees. Hidden fees. Every time you buy shares in a mutual fund, a portion of that money goes to fees—sometimes up to 5%. If you employ a standard financial advisor, they charge between 1-2% of the money you have invested with them. Other financial products like annuities and insurance bake in fees that everyday investors like us won't ever hear about.

Here's Jack Bogle again:

> "Active management[94] is going to cost you around 2% all-in for the average fund (including 1.2% average expense ratio, transaction costs, cash drag, and sales charges). **So that means in a 7% market, you'll only get 5%.**"

> "On the contrary, an index fund that costs 0.05% means that you get a 6.95% return. At 6.95%, you turn $1 into about $30 over 50 years. But at 5%, you get $10 instead of $30. And what does that mean? **It means you put up 100% of the cash, you took 100% of the risk, and you got 30% of the reward.** That's what happens when you look at returns over the long term. People don't, but they're going to have to learn to do that."

This is the reason the Stock Market chapter focuses on ETFs and Index Funds with lower fees. If you're invested in mutual funds, here's the truth…

Mutual Funds Suck

Harsh, I know. But someone had to say it.

Mutual funds are actively managed portfolios that are run by a fund manager. They charge fees to pay for the fund manager, who, in turn, is supposed to bring in big returns.

However, the research shows that **virtually no mutual fund managers perform better than simply investing in the entire stock market.**

If you're like me, you learned that mutual funds are safe, diversified

---

[94] Referring to *actively managed* mutual funds.

investments. **Yet, 96% of mutual funds grow *less than* the stock market as a whole.** In finance lingo, they "underperform." For example, the S&P 500 is one measure of the stock market—a basket of 500 of America's largest companies.

If the S&P 500 grows 7% this year, 96% of the mutual funds out there will grow less than 7%. Subtract the hidden fees and they'll do even worse. 4% of mutual funds do beat the market, for a year or two. But if you're hopscotching around trying to find the *best* fund, you're paying even more fees, and chances are you won't. If you're advisor tries to pitch you on *the best* mutual fund, chances are they get a sweet little kick-back from the mutual fund company.

Another financial expert explains mutual funds this way: "I want you to imagine that someone comes to you with the following investment opportunity: he wants you to put up 100% of the capital and take 100% of the risk, and if it makes money, he wants 60% or more of the upside to come to him in fees. Oh, and by the way, if it loses money, you lose, and he still gets paid! Are you in? I'm sure you don't need any time to think this through. It's a no-brainer. Your gut response has to be, "There's no way I'm doing this. How absurd!" The only problem is that if you're like 90% of American investors, you've invested in typical mutual fund, and believe it or not, these are the terms to which you've already agreed. That's right, there is $13 trillion in actively managed mutual funds with 265 million account holders around the world."[xvii]

Uneven Turf

David Swensen, Yale's Chief Investment Officer, is another pro investor who wants to help level the playing field for the average investor:

> **"The fundamental reason that individuals don't have the types of choices they should have is because of the <u>profit orientation in the mutual fund industry</u>.** Don't get me wrong, I'm a capitalist, and I believe in profits. But there's a fundamental conflict between the profit motive and fiduciary

responsibility[95]—because the greater the profits for the [mutual fund], the lower the returns for the investor."

"The problem is that the managers of the mutual funds make more money when they gather huge piles of assets and charge high fees. The high fees are in direct conflict with the goal of producing high returns. And so what happens over and over again is the profits win and the investor seeking returns loses."

"There are only two organizations where that conflict doesn't exist, and they're Vanguard [Jack Bogle mentioned above is the founder] and TIAA-CREF. Both operate on a not-for-profit basis—they're looking out for the investor's interests, and they're strong fiduciaries. And fiduciary responsibility always wins."

"There's another reason the investor's reality is worse than the numbers [96% of mutual funds underperform], and that's because of our own behavioral mistakes we make as individual investors. Individuals tend to buy funds that have good performance. And they chase returns. And then when funds perform poorly, they sell. And so they end up buying high and selling low. **And that's a bad way to make money.**"

So, how in the heck are everyday investors like us supposed to level the playing field? Swensen believes the answer is simple: utilize a long-term buy-and-hold strategy and diversify. He concludes, "I'm not smart enough to know where the markets are going to go."

The good news is that there are ways to ensure your fees are as low as possible while investing in quality funds.

Vanguard is one of the few brokerage firms that is registered as a *fiduciary*. They offer many of the lowest cost funds available to everyday investors. Their funds are often available in your 401k options. If you hire a financial advisor, the maximum percent they should charge you is 1%. Conscious Capital, mentioned in the Advisors chapter, charges between 0.5-1%. Also make sure your advisor is a *fee-only* Registered Investment Advisor (RIA).

---

[95] Defined generally, as the highest standard of care. In investing, a fiduciary responsibility means that someone should have your best financial interests at heart. I mention this in the chapter on Investment Advisors.

The second opportunity to ensure you are paying low fees is to look up the "expense ratio" of the funds you own. The expense ratio represents the fees charged by a fund. A good benchmark is under 0.50% for specialty funds and under 0.20% for funds that simply follow an index, like an S&P 500 ETF. Your 401K should list the expense ratios for each fund. Also, you can use Morningstar, Yahoo! Finance, and many other sites to find the expense ratio. It will be listed in the summary section.

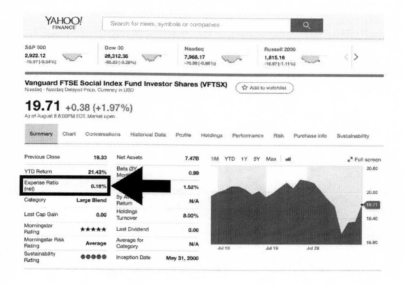

Investing Primer—Review

Successful investing is no longer reserved for "finance people." You have to tools and skills to grow your money, building wealth for you and the people and things you love.

Investing simplified is as easy as **"Start early. Diversify like a pro. Avoid fees."**

Now that you're up to speed on the fundamental rules of investing, you're ready to design a world-class portfolio.

The Four Investing Destinations

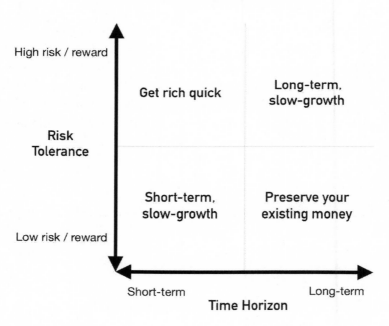

Designing a World-Class Portfolio

A woodsman—a very fine one, I'm sure—was once asked: "What would you do if you had just five minutes to chop down a tree?"

They answered, "I would spend the first two and a half minutes sharpening my axe."

While we are wired for instant gratification, **investing is more like felling a tree with a few well-aimed swings of a razor-sharp axe**.

The chapters ahead are the two and a half minutes of axe sharpening. We'll analyze portfolios designed by some of the best investors in the world. More importantly, you'll find portfolios for any investing situation. Finally, we'll look at these portfolios with the lens of do-gooder investing and see just how impactful and meaningful we can make them.

Start with Why

Why? just might be the greatest question in the world. Ask it anytime and you'll learn something. Better yet, you'll cut through the fluff and go straight to the heart of something.

So *why* are you investing?

"Because my dad told me to."

"Darren in HR made a $100K on Snapchat's IPO."

"It made Warren Buffet a billionaire…"

But *why?* Do you want financial freedom in 20 years? Do you want to feel responsible for your future? Do you want to give your kids and others you love amazing opportunities?

I believe all of us want to serve something greater than ourselves. When we truly listen, there's a desire deep inside of us to be of service. It's part of who we are and is in everything we do. When we listen, it's true of investing, too. Scrooge McDuck could backstroke in his money pool, but is that what you really want?

Do you want to pass money on to your children and grandchildren? Vote with your dollars? Make positive change? Bend the arc of history for the better?

Personally, *I* invest because I desire financial freedom for my family, the opportunity to see the world, and the capacity to influence the movement towards a happier, healthier, balanced planet.

Instead of investing because *you're supposed to*, let your true desires guide your investing. This will inform where you want to go and how to get there.

Where do you want to go?

"Waze, take me to a restaurant." Said no one, ever.

Waze can alert you to potholes, crashes, and a hidden police car, but it still needs to know where you want to go. Otherwise you'll end up at A Restaurant, 3334 West Coast Hwy, Newport Beach, CA 92663. Maybe a true story.

Once you know why you invest, you can determine where you want to go. *Where* has four general destinations.

The Four Investing Destinations

The Four Investing Destinations can be determined by two primary criteria: time horizon and risk tolerance.

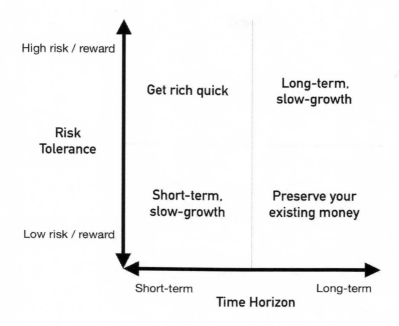

The four investing destinations are:

1. Get rich quick
2. Long-term, slow-growth
3. Preserve your existing money
4. Short-term, slow-growth

Here's a quick look at each investing destination to help guide you to understand which destination applies to you. Keep in mind, you can have multiple destinations, e.g. money set aside for long-term, slow-growth needs, and money that you plan to use soon with short-term, slow-growth needs.

Get rich quick

This destination features high-risk, short-term investing in *hopes* of turning a little money into a lot of money quickly. Strategies include trading options, day trading, flipping houses, lottery tickets, and boarding the Black Pearl with Captain Jack Sparrow with sails set for the Treasure of Cortes.

Unless you're an expert, or a pirate, these tactics are highly improbable at producing overnight riches. I'm neither, so weigh anchor and hoist the mizzen!

Long-Term, Slow-Growth

If you are investing for the long-term, don't need the money for a while, and are willing to invest in some higher-risk investments, this is your destination. Long-term investing generally includes a time horizon of 10-40+ years.

Common goals include:
- Retirement
- A young child's college tuition
- Pass on money to your children or grandchildren
- Legacy donation to a school or non-profit later in life

Long-term, slow-growth investing can take on some higher-risk investments because there is time to make up for any losses from those investments.

Preserve Your Existing Money

If you are investing for the long-term but cannot afford to lose the money you've built up, this is likely your destination.

For example, when many people reach retirement, they rely on a steady stream of income from their sizable retirement savings and don't want to risk it to market fluctuations. Typically, they shift to bond and fixed-return investments that are much lower risk. Pro tip: typical investing advice offers the 4% Rule to help guide how much money you'll need at retirement. A portfolio invested in relatively safe bonds can produce a fixed-income of 4% per year that you can live off of, without eating into the principal of your retirement account. For example, a $1,000,000 account invested in 4%-yield bonds will produce about $40,000 per year in interest alone.

Now, the 4% Rule could be amended to the 3.5% Rule because bond interest rates are not what they once were. However, as you've seen throughout the book, there are quite a few fixed-return investments that pay more than 4%.

Common goals include:

- Existing nest egg built up for retirement that will be your main source of income (if it takes a big down swing, it could dramatically alter your retirement)
- Money set aside for a downpayment or college tuition in the future (5+ years) that you really do not want to lose

Short-term, Slow-growth

If you are investing money that you will need in the next five years and you don't want to risk losing it, this is the destination for that money.

Common goals include:

- House downpayment
- College tuition
- Grad school tuition
- Moving to a new location
- Starting a business

Two important factors that impact short-term investing are liquidity and inflation. Liquidity refers to your ability to access your money. If you know you'll need the money in one year, you don't want to put it in an investment that locks it up for five years. Inflation is the increase in the cost of stuff, like housing, gas, and tacos.[96] If you're planning to buy a house in five years, but your money is parked in a low-yield savings account, you could be losing value. I'll show you some strategies to keep pace with inflation for short-term, slow-growth investments in this chapter.

Creating Positive Impact

In addition to growing or preserving your money, you can use a do-gooder's lens to create positive impact for your portfolio. Do-gooder investing is on a spectrum from 0% do-gooder to 100% do-gooder.

---

[96] Taco inflation has consistently outpaced average inflation for five years running. Alas, I could not find a taco ETF to invest in, otherwise I would.

The Do-Gooder Investing Spectrum

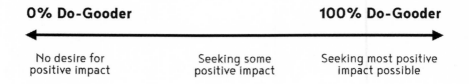

0% Do-Gooder

100% Do-Gooder

No desire for
positive impact

Seeking some
positive impact

Seeking most positive
impact possible

In the chapters ahead, we'll look at each destination with a do-gooder's lens, with the goal of mimicking or improving upon conventional investments.

Get a Life

One final note: You have a life. I have a life. Does financial success mean we have to spend it crunching numbers?

Peter Lynch, a legendary investor whose book *One Up on Wall Street* inspired me two decades ago, said, "If you spend more than 13 minutes analyzing economic and market forecasts, you've wasted 10 minutes."

If I've done my job well—and you do your job of setting up your investment strategies—you should be able to check your investments twice a year, do a little shimmy while you rebalance, and get back to living.

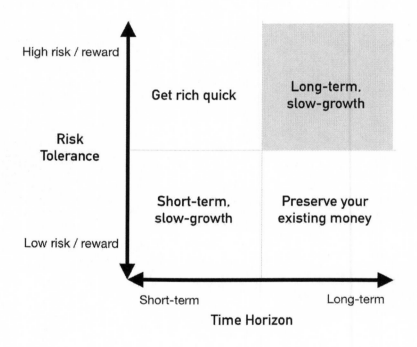

Long-term, Slow-growth Investing

In this chapter, we'll discuss how to invest successfully for the long-term. First, let's take a look at how the best investors in the world grow their money. Then, it's time to apply our knowledge of do-gooder investments to create a portfolio that's profitable and purposeful. Here's an example of a portfolio that can do both.

70% Do-Gooder All-Weather Portfolio

% of Total Long-Term Investments	Investment
30% Stocks	Vanguard FTSE Social Index (VFTSX)
40% Long-Term Bonds	American Homeowner Preservation Columbia U.S. Social Bond Fund (CONAX)
15% Intermediate Term Bonds	iShares 7 – 10 Year Treasury ETF (IEF)
7.5% Gold	SPDR Gold Shares ETF (GLD)
7.5% Commodities	PowerShares DB Commodity Index (DBC) Invesco Solar ETF (TAN)

If this portfolio looks out-of-the-ordinary to you, that's because it is. It's not a typical Stock/Bond asset allocation we discussed in the Investing Primer. This portfolio is an *all-weather* strategy based on a portfolio from one of the world's top investors. The seven investment funds are a mix of conventional investments like a gold ETF and more sustainable investments like American Homeowner Preservation (see Affordable Housing chapter) and Vanguard's FTSE Social Index (VFTSX) discussed in the sustainable stock market chapter.

This portfolio scores high on positive impact while positioned to make money in any economic condition. And, just as important, it's made with easy-to-buy funds that everyday investors can buy and rebalance. So, why does an all-weather allocation look so strange and how will it help you make money over the long-term?

Balance Isn't What You Think

In 2008, when the stock market recessed into a damn-that-hurt black hole, "balanced" portfolios dropped between 25% and 40%.[97] Ouch. "Balanced" portfolios are an investing style that allocates 50% of its money to stocks and 50% to bonds.

Ray Dalio, a top investor you'll meet shortly, exclaims, "With a fifty-fifty portfolio, you really have more like 95% of your *risk* in stocks!"[xviii] Why? **Stocks are 300% more volatile than bonds.**

Most off-the-shelf investing advice and 401K default settings will hand you some version of a "balanced" portfolio. Some percent in stocks, some percent in bonds.

Like a lingering carpet stain, this old school advice is still hanging around. But balanced portfolios are actually riskier than expected. You deserve better.

> Note: If you've been investing with a "balanced" allocation for a long time and it works for you, stick with it. You'll take some hits, like 2008. Your returns will underperform by a little. But if it's easier for you, stick with it. You can still upgrade the sustainability of your funds even if you don't shift to an all-weather approach.

---

[97] The only reason I made it through this period without panicking is because I was trekking around China and riding horses in Mongolia and forgot about my investments.

The all-weather portfolios ahead aren't complicated, but they require a rewiring of your understanding of risk. I find that many people who've been conditioned to a Stocks/Bonds portfolio their entire lives have a hard time swallowing a new methodology. But if you're open to exploring, I'll walk you through how all-weather diversifies risk and return across the four economic seasons ahead.

All-Weather Investing

What if you could diversify your portfolio so it reduces risk in every economic season, while still growing in good seasons? As a natural-born skeptic, I'll admit it does sound too good to be true. But thanks to investors who manage billions of dollars and want to reduce their volatility without missing out on growth, we can invest with a strategy that provides stable, slow-growth, long-term investing. This is the purpose of all-weather investing. The reason I'm going into depth about all-weather investing is because every person, regardless of their investing experience and income, should have access to top-of-the-line strategies and advice.

So how does all-weather investing differ from off-the-shelf "balanced" portfolios? Balance isn't what you think. To an outsider, a yogi in tree pose might seem like they have "great balance." In reality, the pose demands more: focus, relaxation, breathing, and just the right amount of tensed booty.

All-weather investing is more than balance, too. It's the right mix of focus, historical analysis, patience, and…well…just the right amount of tensed booty.

All-weather investing spreads the risk and volatility of each asset class more evenly than tradition Stock/Bond portfolios. The goal: grow steadily and not lose money.[98]

The goal of all-weather investing is to grow your money in every economic season, skip out on big downturns, and allow for more compounding than a conventional portfolio.

Conventional advice recommends that young people invest *aggressively*, even if it means taking financial punches like 2008. But what if you could

---

[98] They *can* lose money, but they are designed to lose as little as possible.

weather those downturns without losing money? All the more to compound on. Remember, if your portfolio loses 50% of its value, it has to earn 100% to get back to the same spot.

Here's a quick look at an all-weather portfolio we will dissect in a moment. You'll notice it only invests 30% in stocks, 55% in bonds, and 15% in atypical asset classes.

% Portfolio	Dalio's All-Weather Allocation
30%	Stocks
40%	Long-Term Treasury
15%	Intermediate-Term Bonds
7.5%	Gold
7.5%	Commodities

I Wanna Be Like Ray

When I was a kid, I wanted to be like Mike. Now I wanna be like Ray.[99]

Ray Dalio is the Lebron James of investing. He is the founder of Bridgewater Associates, an investment firm with $150 billion under management. Ray has spent 50+ years managing money for folks like the World Bank and advising treasury secretaries. When you're managing massive amounts of money, the last thing you want to do is watch the money shrivel up in a recession. After experiencing world events that triggered economic seasons—decoupling of gold and the U.S. dollar, sky-high interest rates, hostage crises, and dotcom bubbles—Dalio scoured his data to see if he could construct an asset allocation that would be more consistent and reliable. Here's what Ray has to say about this "aha" moment:[100]

---

[99] Sorry Mike.

[100] If you want to learn more about this, grab Ray's tome *Principles*, which discusses his principles for life and investing. Dense and insightful.

"From my earlier failures, I knew that no matter how confident I was in making anyone bet I could still be wrong — and that proper diversification was the key to reducing risks without reducing returns. If I could build properly diversified (they zigged and zagged in ways that balanced each other out), I could offer clients an overall portfolio return much more consistent and reliable than what they could get elsewhere."

"I saw that with fifteen to twenty good, uncorrelated return streams, I could dramatically reduce my risks without reducing my expected returns. It was so simple but it would be such a breakthrough if the theory worked as well in practice as it did on paper. I called it the "Holy Grail of Investing" because it showed the path to making a fortune."

"I worked with Bob and Dan to pull our best decision rules from the pile. Once we had them, we back-tested them over long time frames, using the systems to simulate how the decision rules would have worked together in the past..."

"We were startled by the results. On paper, this new approach improved our returns by a factor of three to five times per unit of risk, and we could calibrate the amount of return we wanted based on the amount of risk we could tolerate. In other words, we could make a ton more money than the other guys, with a lower risk of being knocked out of the game—as I'd nearly been before."

Dalio's new understanding of asset allocation was dubbed the All-Weather Portfolio because, instead of trying to predict what economic conditions are coming next, it grows in all economic weather conditions.

So, how'd it do? When many investment portfolios plummeted 40% in 2008, the All-Weather Portfolio dropped just 3.9%. [Finger snaps!]

Dissecting Ray Dalio's All-Weather Portfolio

Thankfully, the investing world is highly scrutinized. Tell someone you only lost 3.9% in one of the toughest recessions in history and they're going to check your math. Here is the performance of Dalio's All-Weather Portfolio backtested from 1984 to 2013:

- 9.7% annual returns (*with* fees subtracted)
- You would have made money 86% of the time (so only four down years)
- Average loss of just 1.9% in those years
- Worst loss was -3.9%
- Volatility was 7.6%

In Part 1, a historical look at the returns of the general stock market showed returns of about 7.7% after fees. If you had invested $100,000 in an S&P 500 mutual fund in 1984 and added $5,000 every year until 2013, your money would have grown to about $1,390,000. A "balanced" portfolio would have returned less.

Dalio's portfolio—with a 2% higher return—would have netted you over $2,200,000, almost one million dollars more, while skipping out on the drastic peaks and valleys of typical investing.

Perhaps more important than its upward performance is the portfolio's record of *not losing money*, even during big crashes. Warren Buffet's number one rule for investing is "Don't lose money" and this portfolio does just that.

I believe this deserves the first-ever haiku about all-weather investing.

Don't risk your money
Let it grow long, lazy, slow
Go with all-weather

Replicating The All-Weather

Everyday investors can replicate this portfolio using these traditional (i.e. not necessarily do-gooder) low-cost funds:[101]

---

[101] Note: This is not the exact same strategy as Bridgewater's All-Weather Fund, which uses ultra-fancy investments and may borrow money to maximize returns. But these are the percentages designed directly by Ray and the lowest cost ETFs in each asset class.

% of Total Long-Term Investments	Investment
30% Stocks	Vanguard Total Stock Market ETF (VTI)
40% Long-Term Bonds	iShares 20+ Year Treasury ETF (TLT)
15% Intermediate Term Bonds	iShares 7-10 Year Treasury ETF (IEF)
7.5% Gold	SPDR Gold Shares ETF (GLD)
7.5% Commodities	PowerShares DB Commodity Index Tracking Fund (DBC)

We'll take a look at how this performs on do-gooder measurement ahead.

David Swensen's Lazy Portfolio

Another money master—David Swensen—invests using a similar all-weather approach, dubbed the Lazy Portfolio.

David Swensen is Yale's Chief Investment Officer and author of *Unconventional Success*, a book about his contrarian investment approach. He's responsible for taking Yale's endowment from $1 billion to $23 billion with a long-term, slow-growth, don't-lose-money approach. Swensen's commentary in the Investing Primer chapter urges everyday investors to steer clear of mutual funds and keep fees low to help level the playing field.

Swensen's allocation is very diversified, underweighted in stocks compared to most balanced portfolios, and emphasizes low-cost funds. His portfolio, while more volatile than Dalio's, has performed very well over the years and can be replicated with these conventional, low-cost funds:

% of Total Long-Term Investments	Investment
30% Stocks	Vanguard Total Stock Mkt Index (VTSMX)
20% Real Estate Index	Vanguard REIT Index Fund (VGSIX)
15% Long-Term Treasury	Vanguard Long-Term Treasury Fund Inv (VUSTX)
15% Foreign Developed Markets	Vanguard Developed Markets Index Fund (VDVIX)
15% Treasury Inflation Protected Securities (TIPS)	Vanguard Inflation-Protected Securities Fund Investor Shares (VIPSX)
5% Emerging Markets	Vanguard Emerging Markets Stock Index Fund (VEIEX)

Rain or Shine

Before modifying these portfolios to make them more sustainable, it's helpful to understand why these all-weather portfolios do so well.

**Note: This section is going to get into the weeds. If you generally understand the three core reasons for an all-weather approach, you're all good.

Dalio and Swensen are smart. So smart they know they can't predict the market. Their all-weather portfolios perform well, rain or shine, for three reasons.
1. More than Balanced, Ready for Every Season
2. Rebalancing
3. Low fees

All-Weather Secret #1—More than Balanced, Ready for Every Season

Four things determine how different investments perform:
1. Increasing inflation
2. Decreasing inflation (deflation)
3. Increasing economic growth
4. Decreasing economic growth

When combined, they create four economic "seasons." Here's a visualization:

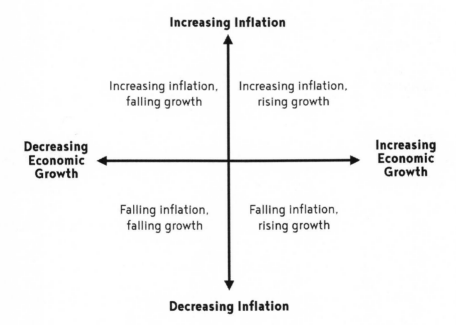

Increasing Inflation

Increasing inflation, falling growth | Increasing inflation, rising growth

Decreasing Economic Growth ←→ **Increasing Economic Growth**

Falling inflation, falling growth | Falling inflation, rising growth

Decreasing Inflation

The economy will be in one of these four economic conditions at any given time. But, since we don't always know which season we are in or what season is coming next, it's hard to pick the perfect investments for each season. The uniqueness of the all-weather approach means we can design a portfolio that will do well in five years, even though we have no idea what the economic conditions will be in five years (or twenty years, for that matter).

An all-weather strategy attempts to balance investments across the economic seasons. It assigns 25% of your risk in each of the economic conditions. (Remember, stocks are 300% more volatile than bonds). The table below shows which investments perform well in each condition.

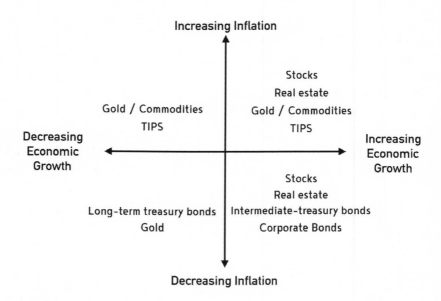

An all-weather portfolio is prepared for any season and allocates its investments accordingly.

That's why Ray Dalio's portfolio grew during the Lost Decade—from the beginning of 2000 to the end of 2009—when the S&P 500's returns were flat (well, up and then *down*, but no growth for the decade). **During the Lost Decade, an all-weather portfolio would have grown 80%, while owning a portfolio with only stocks returned 0%.**

And from 2000 to 2015, an all-weather allocation grew 200%, turning $100,000 into $300,000, while the S&P 500 grew 90%, turning $100,000 into $190,000.

This is definitely a trip into the weeds, but I hope it illuminates the wisdom in these portfolios. After all, you've worked hard for your money. Why not let it work hard for you? Keep in mind that the all-weather portfolios proposed are not meant to be a perfect solution for every investor. My intent is to offer rarely considered insight into diversification across the four major economic conditions.

All-Weather Secret #2—Rebalance

The backtesting on the portfolios listed above include annual rebalancing (discussed in the Investing Primer chapter). Annual rebalancing realigns the allocation—e.g. if stocks grew over the year and now make up 35% of the portfolio, rebalancing sells the proportion of stocks that brings them back to the target allocation of 30%.

All-Weather Secret #3—Low Fees

Swensen's Lazy Portfolio all-weather strategy relies on low fees offered by Index funds and ETFs. As discussed earlier, lower fees add up to higher yearly earnings and more money for compounding. Over the long term, this makes a big difference on earnings.

Sustainability and Long-Term Investing

Can the best get even better? While it's undeniable Swensen and Dalio are top-notch investors, they entered the investing world during a time before our planet was losing 10 species per day. Before air pollution killed millions. Before the water crisis threatened our way of life.

The world is changing—and it's in need of investing strategies that grow money while increasing equity and balancing people with planet. Whether Swensen and Dalio are updating their investment strategies for a resource constrained world, I don't know. But I do know other world-class investors are making big changes. In 2016, the Bill & Melinda Gates Foundation, with over $40 billion invested, *divested* from owning fossil fuel company stocks. They joined over 1,000 large wealth funds who have committed to divest their portfolios from fossil fuel companies. You can find the top fossil fuel-free funds in the A More Sustainable Stock Market chapter.

Moral and ethical commitments aren't the only factors driving the shift to more responsible investments for long-term investors. Professional investors are considered fiduciaries—a person who holds a legal position of trust. In investing terms, they are obligated to do what's best for the people they manage money for. Regulators like the G20 Financial Stability Board's Task Force on Climate-Related Financial Disclosures are now explicit that *climate change* and the threat of stranded fossil fuel assets pose a significant risk to investor value, and that fiduciaries have a legal duty to manage that risk through divestment and other strategies.

In 2015, Morgan Stanley reviewed over 10,000 open-end mutual funds and found over the previous 15 years sustainable funds tended to exhibit slightly higher returns and lower volatility than their traditional counterparts.[xix]

Investors must ask themselves two questions: 1) Which investments are going to do best in a resource-constrained future? 2) What is the type of future I want to help build?

Scoring All-Weather for Sustainability

After grading Dalio and Swensen's investments with Morningstar's Sustainability Rating, they scored less than do-gooder. Swensen's portfolio averaged a sustainability rating of 2.75 out of 5. Dalio's scored a 2 out of 5.[102] You're killing me, Dals!

Long-term, Slow-growth Investing for Do-Gooders

Can we find investments that fit into an all-weather asset allocation, perform well, *and* have positive impact on the world? Using the following criteria, I created two sustainable portfolios designed for long-term, slow-growth and high positive impact.

Do-gooder Criteria
- Historical performance comparable to other investments in the same asset class (meaning, I'm not going to recommend an ETF that returned 4% when the S&P returned 8%)
- High positive impact score
- Low fees

---

[102] Scoring tables located online.

For example, the long-term treasury bond fund (TLT) used in the original Dalio allocation returned 5.8% per year over the last 15 years. Using this as a guide, I included options that would provide similar returns to this long-term bond fund. In the first Long-Term Portfolio 1 ahead, these options include investments like American Homeowner Preservation (AHP) and Small Change that deliver higher returns than a bond fund and are not tied to the stock market regarding their returns. So, in this sense, these do-gooder options do not exactly replicate the long-term treasury bond asset class, but they are less risky.

To see a full spreadsheet of investments, including their impact scores, fees, and performance, go to www.adrianreif.com/dogoodersguide

All-Weather, Upgraded for Impact

The following tables show high-impact options for each asset class in Ray Dalio's All-Weather Portfolio and the investment's impact score (1-5, 5 being highest). If you plan to replicate the all-weather strategy with these high-impact, choose at least one from each table.[103]

Do-Gooder Long-Term Portfolio 1

% Portfolio	Dalio's All-Weather Allocation
30%	Stocks
40%	Long-Term Treasury
15%	Intermediate-Term Bonds
7.5%	Gold
7.5%	Commodities

---

[103] As you'll see in the upcoming chapter—Real World Portfolios—you can portion these to your tastes. For example, if you have $100,000 invested, you can invest 40% in long-term bonds with $20,000 in iShares 20+ Year Treasury ETF (Dalio's original) and $20,000 in American Homeowner Preservation, one of our sustainable substitutes.

30% Stocks—Do Gooder Options	Impact Score
Vanguard FTSE Social Index (VFTSX)	5
Vanguard PRIMECAP Inv (VPMCX)	5
USA ESG Select ETF (SUSA)	5
KLD 400 Social ETF (DSI)	5
Aspiration Redwood Fund (REDWX)	5
PAX Elevate Global Women's Leadership (PXWEX)	5
S&P 500 Fossil Fuel Free ETF (SPYX)	5
ETHO Climate Leadership ETF (ETHO)	4
Pattern Energy Group (PEGI)	5
Brookfield Renewable Partners (BEP)	5
40% Long-Term Bonds—Do Gooder Options	**Impact Score**
American Homeowner Preservation (AHP)	5
Small Change	5
Columbia U.S. Social Bond Fund Class A (CONAX)	5
Same as original*	2.5
15% Interm Bonds—Do Gooder Options	**Impact Score**
Columbia U.S. Social Bond Fund Class A (CONAX)	4
Domini Social Bond Fund (DSBFX)	3
Organic Valley Preferred Stock	5
Same as original*	2.5
7.5% Gold—Do Gooder Options	**Impact Score**
The Reinvestment Fund	5
Clean Energy Credit Union CD	5
Calvert Community Investment Note	5
Same as original*	2.5
7.5% Commodities—Do Gooder Options	**Impact Score**
Guggenheim Solar ETF (TAN)	5
Pattern Energy Group (PEGI)	5
Same as original*	0

*"Same as original" denoted because the original treasury funds have minimal positive or negative sustainable impact, but they provide great diversification.

Do-Gooder Long-Term Portfolio 2

The following set of tables show high-impact options for each asset class in David Swensen's Lazy Portfolio and the investment's impact score (1-5, 5 being highest).

**Note: This portfolio is likely enhanced by ESG / sustainable options in those classes listed below because, according to Morningstar, sustainability provided even higher performance benefits for companies in foreign developed markets and emerging markets.

% Portfolio	Swensen's Lazy Allocation
30%	US Stocks
20%	Real Estate
15%	Long-Term Treasury
15%	Foreign Developed Stocks
15%	Treasure Inflation Protected Securities
5%	Emerging Market Stocks

30% Stocks—Do Gooder Options	Impact Score
See Portfolio 1 Stock options	5

20% Real Estate—Do Gooder Options	Impact Score
American Homeowner Preservation (AHP)	5
Small Change	5
Digital Realty (DLR)	4
Envest Microfinance	5

15% LT Treasury Bonds—Do Gooder Options	Impact Score
Columbia U.S. Social Bond Fund Class A (CONAX)	4
Organic Valley Preferred Stock	5
Same as original*	2.5

15% Foreign Developed Stock—Do Gooder Options	Impact Score
Xtrackers ESG Leaders ETF (EASG)	5
Vanguard PRIMECAP Inv (VPMCX)	5
Calvert International Equity (CWVGX)	5

15% TIPS—Do Gooder Options	Impact Score
The Reinvestment Fund	5
Calvert Community Investment Note	5
Same as original*	2.5

5% Emerging Market Stocks—Do Gooder Options	Impact Score
iShares ESG Emerging Markets ETF (ESGE)	4
Calvert Emerging Markets Equity (CVMAX)	4
New Alternatives Fund (NALFX)	4

*Same as original denoted because the original treasury funds have minimal positive or negative sustainable impact, but they provide great diversification.

Do-Gooder Long-Term Portfolio 3

Of course, Goldilocks didn't eat just any porridge—she made sure to find the one that's just right. You should do the same for your portfolio. The next portfolios is an example of a blended portfolio that uses some of the original investments from Dalio's all-weather approach, like the iShares 20+ Year Treasury ETF, which I really like because it stabilizes the portfolio when economic growth slows. But it also features great social impact investments like American Homeowner Preservation (AHP), Invesco Solar ETF, and Working Capital for Community Needs that can help you align your investments with your values.

It is depicted as a hypothetical $1 million total balance so you can see how the dollar amounts are spread across traditional and do-gooder investments.

Blended All-Weather Portfolio

This portfolio is an all-weather approach that is slightly more growth oriented. It contains a mix of traditional, status quo investments and high-impact, high-performance investments from this book. The result is a portfolio designed to grow slowly and in every economic season while creating positive impact, like investing in companies that have more women on their boards and executive positions, supporting renewable energy growth, affordable housing development, helping build up low-income communities, and taking advantage of the future growth in solar energy. The portfolio's impact score is 3.9 out of 5.

30% Stocks—Do Gooder Options	Impact Score	$ Amount
Vanguard Total Stock Market ETF	3	$100k
USA ESG Select ETF	5	$100k
PAX Elevate Global Women's Leadership	5	$100k
20% Long-Term Treasury	Impact Score	$ Amount
iShares 20+ Year Treasury ETF	2.5	$200k
20% Real Estate—Do Gooder Options	Impact Score	$ Amount
Pattern Energy Group	5	$50k
American Homeowner Preservation	5	$100k
Small Change	5	$50k
15% Interm Bonds + Do Gooder	Impact Score	$ Amount
iShares 7-10 Year Treasury ETF	2.5	$75k
Neighborly Municipal Bonds	4	$75k
7.5% Gold + Do Gooder Options	Impact Score	$ Amount
SPDR Gold Shares ETF	2.5	$25k
The Reinvestment Fund	5	$50k
7.5% Commodities + Do Gooder	Impact Score	$ Amount
PowerShares DB Commodity Index Fund (DBC)	2.5	$25k
Invesco Solar ETF (TAN)	5	$25k
Working Capital for Community Needs (WCCN)	5	$25k

Swensen or Dalio?

When compared side-by-side, you can see there are differences in Dalio's all-weather approach and Swensen's lazy approach.

Dalio	Asset Class	Swensen
30%	Stocks	50%
40%	LT Treasury Bonds	15%
15%	IT Treasury Bonds	0%
0%	TIPS	15%
0%	Real Estate	20%
15%	Gold / Commodities	0%

If you're having trouble deciding between these two simple asset allocations, here some checkpoints:

The Swensen allocation is a bit more growth-oriented. It dropped 22% in 2008, while the Dalio allocation was down 3.9% the same year. If you are earlier in your career, don't mind added volatility / risk, and believe the stock market (along with foreign markets) are going to continue to perform really well, then the Swensen allocation is more your style.

The Dalio allocation is designed to be consistent and reliable, not take big losses even in recession years, and grow steadily. If you enjoy taking less risk, are mid-career or even nearing retirement, and won't need all of your money for some time, the Dalio portfolio will suit you. (If you're nearing retirement or in it and really want to protect your nest egg, check out the Preserve Your Existing Money chapter.)

Now that you've mastered long-term investing, let's look at short-term investing.

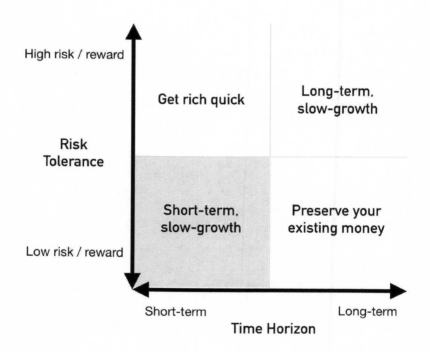

Short-Term, Slow-Growth Investing

If you are investing money that you will need in the next five years, this is the destination for that money. Short-term investing is useful for planned spending like a down payment on a house, college tuition, or a child's wedding. Or you might be setting aside an emergency savings account with enough money to cover a year of expenses (like many money gurus recommend).

Short-term investing demands different requirements than long-term investing, especially if you do not want to risk losing the money. Here are three criteria for successful short-term investing.

1. Lower risk
2. Liquidity & timeframe
3. Keep pace with inflation

#1—Lower Risk

Let's say you know within the next two years you plan to put a down payment on a house. If that money is invested in stocks or bonds, a market downturn could seriously impact your plans. Predicting the future is impossible and you don't want to leave your money to the whim of the market. Low-risk means the investments are unlikely to take big swings.

#2—Liquidity & Timeframe

Liquid is fluid. It can move anywhere. Liquidity is a fancy term that means your money is readily accessible. Liquidity is important for short-term investing so you can ensure you can receive it to pay for your planned expenses.

Some investments are locked in for a period of time, while others are immediately accessible. For example, it may take you several months to sell your house and use the money. Other investments like CDs are locked in for a period of time, sometimes five years.

The key is knowing when you will need your money and planning your short-term investments accordingly. For example, if you know grad school tuition is due in three years, you can invest in an investment with a two or three year term.

#3—Keep Pace with Inflation

Over the last 10 years, inflation averaged 1.7% per year. This means a $10 widget cost 17 cents more every year.

At the time of writing, the average savings account in the U.S. pays out 0.09% in interest per year. If you have a significant amount of short-term money sitting in a low-yield savings account, your money is losing value. For example, if you have $100,000 in a savings account with 0.09% interest it would grow to $100,270 in three years (while the cost of living has increased even more). If the interest rate were a modest 2%, your ending balance after three years would be $106,178—a difference of $6,000.[104]

Short-term investing, when done right, can grow your money and *keep pace* with inflation. The good news is there are several banks that offer meaningful interest rates while creating positive impact.

Adrian's Favorite Short-term Do-Gooder Investments

Short-term do-gooder investing isn't anything special. The examples below combine your need for lower risk, liquidity options, and modest interest rates with high-impact organizations making the world a better place.

Short-term savings | CNote offers a 2.75% interest rate at the time of writing. Your balance is accessible every 3 months. CNote lends money primarily to women-owned and minority-owned businesses. See the Investing in Communities & Poverty Alleviation chapter for more information.

---

[104] I'm not a proponent of chasing the highest interest rate from bank to bank, but the difference between the average rate and other low-risk investments can be important for the average person.

High-Interest Savings Account | Aspiration's online savings account offers an interest rate above the inflation rate with a debit card and easy transfers to and from other bank accounts. See Banking for Good Chapter.

Favorite Bank | I run my business account with Amalgamated Bank, a B Corporation committed to 100% renewable energy. They help finance affordable housing, are first-movers on social issues, and offers free accounts with reasonable interest rates. See Banking for Good chapter.

High-Impact, Short-Term Investment | RSF Social Investment Fund lends directly to healthy food system entrepreneurs, has a 90-day term, and allows you to participate in the community pricing gatherings— e.g. you help determine interest rates charged to lendees. How's that for collaboration?

Summary of Short-term Investments

The table ahead lists investments from this book with short-term options, from 90 days up to 5 years. Note: Rates will change.[105]

**While keeping pace with inflation is an important factor, some of these investments earn less than inflation. I include them because I know investors who choose to put their money to work in these compelling and meaningful organizations, and believe that missing a percent or two on returns is worth it. Each of you has the good fortune to make sure own decisions.

---

[105] If you email me about a rate change, I'll reply "Yes, I said 'Rates will change' 33 times in this book." You'll probably reply and say, "Dude, I counted and you only said it 24 times. How could you?" I'll reply, "Hey, you're awesome, but you missed the one in this footnote. That's 25. Boom!" Then we'll become best friends.

Organization	Impact Area	Min. Investment	Target Returns	Term
Amalgamated Bank Savings Account	Responsible lending, Union-owned, Renewable energy powered	$1	1.60%	1 day
Aspiration Savings and Checking	Responsible Banking	$10	2%	1 day
Good Money	Responsible Banking	$10	4%	1 day
CNote	Women & Minority-owned businesses	$1	2.75%	90 days
RSF Social Investment Fund Note	Food System	$1,000	1%	90 days
NatureVest Conservation Note	Nature	$25,000	0.80%/ 2.00%	1 / 5 years
Enterprise Community Partners	Affordable Housing	$5,000	0.85%/ 2.5%	1 / 5 years
Calvert Community Investment Note	Communities	$25	1%/2%	1 / 5 years
Affordable Homes of South Texas	Affordable Housing	$100	1.5%/ 3%	1 / 5 year
Iroquois Valley Farms Soil Restoration Note	Nature, Food System	$25,000	1.50%	1 year
Iroquois Valley Farms Soil Restoration Note (Non-Accredited)	Nature, Food System	$25,000	1.50%	1 year
Reinvestment Fund	Communities	$1,000	1.75%/ 2.25%	3 / 6 years
Working Capital for Community Needs (WCCN)	Microfinance	$1,000	2%/4%	2 years
Clean Energy Credit Union CD	Renewable Energy	$1,000	2.80%	5 years
Envest	Microfinance	$25,000	5%	2 years

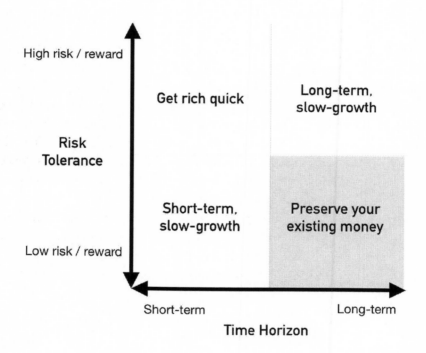

Preserve Your Money

If you are investing for the long-term but cannot afford to lose the money you've built up, this is likely your destination. A strategy for preserving your existing money relies on lower-risk investments. However, your portfolio may include investments with higher returns thanks to the longer time frame.

One example that relies on a preservation strategy is retirement. Once retired, a person may need income for another 30 years. With life extension and health advances, who knows how much longer the average lifespan could become. Most people will rely on the money they've saved (and invested!) throughout their life (remember, get started early!). If played right, that money could finance your life until you kick the bucket. Of course, many people also want to pass money on to their children, loved ones, or a favorite organization after they pass away, so preserving your money is even more important if this is the case.

Many advisors and online calculators can help you forecast your income and expenses during retirement. If you're not savvy with spreadsheets, I highly recommend receiving professional guidance.

Here are the criteria that make up a sound preservation of wealth strategy.

1. Know your risk
2. Generate income
3. Diversify

#1—Know Your Risk

It's possibly more important to zero in on your risk level later in life than earlier. In short, you have less time to make up any big losses. Some finance gurus suggest keeping a portion of a preservation-style portfolio in stocks in hopes of a little extra growth over time. In your case, make sure you are OK with this. Remember, stocks can move up and down without notice.

You don't want to be caught in a downturn when you rely on your money for living.

However, many folks receive social security payments (that hopefully will continue) as part of their income in retirement and may not rely solely on their investment portfolio for income. If this is you, you may be able to take a little more risk.

#2—Generate Income

If your investment portfolio is the main source of your income, you'll want to find investments that yield at least 3% and higher.

Conventional financial wisdom will turn this into a 100% bond portfolio, which assumes less risk and could pay you 3.5% per year on your balance. Generally, the higher return you seek, the higher the risk. Several of the do-gooder investments listed ahead are unique because they provide substantial income—up to 10%—while not being linked to market movements.

#3-Diversify

One pitfall of investing in a 100% bond portfolio—or 100% of any one thing—is the bond market could drop and 100% of your money would drop with it.

Preserving wealth over the long term demands a good diversification strategy. You might allocate a portion of your low-risk investments to bonds, real estate, and affordable housing.

Adrian's Favorite Preservation Do-Gooder Investments

The examples below are a few of my favorite investments that can provide consistent income, low risk, and high-social impact.

High-Yield Affordable Housing | American Homeowner Preservation (AHP) offers a 10% return paid monthly while buying up distressed mortgages and keeping homeowners in their homes. See Affordable Housing chapter for more.

High-Yield Renewable Energy | Wunder Capital's Income Fund pays you 6% per year while financing solar projects for schools and utilities across the U.S. This investment is only for accredited investors, but many retirees will fall into this designation. See Renewable Energy chapter.

Income-Producing Community Investments | Neighborly helps you find municipal bonds—loans made to cities and school districts—that fund libraries, schools, parks, and more. Some bonds on Neighborly pay 4% interest (tax equivalent yield since municipal bonds are tax-free) and are very highly rated, e.g. unlikely to default. See Investing in Communities & Poverty Alleviation chapter.

High-Impact Income | The Reinvestment Fund invests in early childhood centers, affordable housing, grocery stores and more in low-income communities. The longer term notes (10+ years) pay 3.5%-4.5% with almost no risk while creating powerful impact in communities that need it most. See Investing in Communities & Poverty Alleviation chapter.

Microfinance Income | Working Capital for Community Needs (WCCN) pays 3.5%-4% with minimal risk on a four-year term, which is very reasonable, while investing in emerging entrepreneurs around the world. See Microfinance chapter.

A $1.5 million portfolio spread evenly across the previous five investments would produce $84,000 per year in income.

Summary of Preserve Your Existing Money Investments

The investments below are do-gooder investments with medium-to-low risk profiles—they won't fluctuate much or at all—and generate returns from 2.75% to 10%.

Organization	Impact Area	Min. Investment	Target Returns	Term
American Homeowner Preservation (AHP)	Affrodable Housing	$100	10%	5 years
Wunder Capital	Renewable Energy	$1,000	6%	10 years
Reinvestment Fund	Communities	$1,000	4.50%	3-15 years
Neighborly	Communities	$1,000	3%-4%	1-20 years
Working Capital for Community Needs (WCCN)	Microfinance	$1,000	4%	4 years
Enterprise Community Partners	Affordable Housing	$5,000	3.50%	10 years
Calvert Community Investment Note	Communities	$25	4%	1-15 years
Affordable Homes of South Texas	Affordable Housing	$100	3.25%	1-10 years
CNote	Communities	$1	2.75%	90 days
Clean Energy Credit Union CD	Renewable Energy	$1,000	2.80%	5-10 years
Envest	Microfinance	$25,000	6%	2-4 years
Guerrilla Development	Affordable Housing, Real Estate	$3,000	5%	10 years
Saturna Sustainable Bonds	Sustainable Companies	$10,000	2.80%	3 days

The Weird Kids

This chapter is an ode to those of us who've found ways to fit in while unabashedly being ourselves.

Sustainable investing has many weird kids. Investments that don't fit neatly into one of the major asset classes, yet offer outstanding benefits.

One example is the Reinvestment Fund, which invests in under-resourced neighborhoods by funding early childhood education centers, art projects, and affordable housing. Financially, it pays 4.5% interest per year (for the 15-year term) with 100% payback history, making it very low risk. The return is on par with many bonds, but the investment doesn't face the same fluctuations as bond prices, which can move down during certain economic conditions. Should we treat it like a bond? Or a CD?

Here's another example: The YieldCos featured in the Renewable Energy chapter are companies that own large renewable energy generation projects. This means they own tangible assets and have long-term contracts with utilities to buy the electricity they produce. With the price of renewable electricity decreasing and demand for electricity increasing, it seems like the future is bright for these companies. However, their stock prices don't increase (or fluctuate) as much as typical high-growth companies like Google or Apple. When you own the stock you receive a high dividend, from 3% up to 9%. I'm heavily invested in YieldCos because I really like the strong quarterly dividend and I don't have to worry about a huge price drop.[106] I put them in the "Stock" bucket of my all-weather allocation, even though they provide more stability, like bonds.

But what about the weirdest kid of all—and perhaps my favorite investment in the book—American Homeowner Preservations (see Affordable Housing chapter). AHP is an innovative new take on social impact investing. They use funds to buy up homes that would be foreclosed

---

[106] I do keep my eyes on each YieldCo I own to make sure they aren't over-leveraging. I only invest in the top YieldCos, which I denote in the Renewable Energy chapter. You could also invest in a wide variety of YieldCos with Global X YieldCo ETF (YLCO).

on by the banks that own the mortgages. AHP buys the mortgages and instead of kicking out the homeowner, it works with them to develop a sustainable mortgage schedule. Win-win. Their first fund, which is now closed to new investment, offered a 12% dividend. The second fund offers a 10% return.

These weird kids don't fit neatly into a category, which is why many financial advisors don't know about them or won't recommend them. But if you could earn 10% without taking on market fluctuations, would you?

Personally, I like low risk investments and consistent dividend payments. I emphasize seeking risk-adjusted returns, meaning I'm less interested in a 15% return if the risk is very high. I'm happy with a consistent 6% if I'm nearly guaranteed to recoup my investment. Investments like Wunder Capital and the Reinvestment Fund pay out dividends every year, even if the market goes down, and have very limited risk.

Of course, I still invest 30% of my portfolio in large, sustainable companies via ETFs in hopes of reaping long-term growth. But I hope you'll find the sustainable investing world as curiously weird and wonderful as I do, especially as new approaches to creating positive impact unfold.

It turns out the weird kids are going to be OK after all.

Real World Portfolios

Your portfolio is your blank canvas. You can draw lines and paint inside them. You can flick paint from the end of your brush, or even roll in paint and smear your body across the canvas, if your into that sort of thing.[107]

I hate to break it to you, but there's no *"the one."* I'm talking about portfolios, of course. The portfolios in Part 3 are guides. You can follow them to the T. This will put you in good company. You can also modify them or make small adjustments to your existing investment portfolio. Some of you might shift 10% of your current investments from traditional status quo to positive impact investments. If nothing else, at least inspect your 401K and know what you own.

I believe in the power of sustainable investing to help you align your values and your money while creating real, tangible impact in the world. I know many investors who have built 100% sustainable portfolios because they believe this, too.

Ultimately, you get to choose. Determine why you want to invest and *where* you want to go to help you determine how to get there. If you need help, find a fiduciary advisor with an emphasis on sustainable investing. You can use the 7 Questions You Absolutely Must Ask Your Advisor listed in the Investment Advisors chapter to guide you.

Real World Blended Do-Gooder Portfolios

I asked several experienced do-gooder investors—and amazing human beings—to share their portfolios for additional guidance. As you'll see, none of them are the same.

While the portfolios are focused on creating positive impact, they are not 100% do-gooder and for good reason. They meet the individual's needs, investing outlook, and interests, like fixing up old houses. Let's take a look and see how real people are creating real impact.

---

[107] So avante garde.

The engineer with solar-covered rental houses

This portfolio is used by an engineer who invests in affordable rental housing on the side and puts solar panels on them. The properties have appreciated over the years while still keeping them affordable. They also provide income which goes into long-term investing.

The portfolio's impact score is 4.14 out of 5 and could be increased even more by switching to Aspiration or CNote for the high-yield savings and using a Vanguard ESG large-cap ETF for stocks.

Target Allocation %	Investment	Sub-allocation	Impact Score
22.5% Stocks	US Large Cap	22.50%	3
61% Real Estate	4 Residential affordable rental properties (with solar panels)	61.00%	5
6.5% Long-Term Treasury	Series EE Treasury Bonds (direct)	6.50%	2.5
10% Store of value	Cash / High-yield savings	10.00%	2.5

Educator and Investor

This portfolio, based off of the all-weather approach, is used by a person who works in education helping teachers and institutions provide way better education.

The portfolio's impact score is 3.4 out of 5. The impact score could be improved by switching the Vanguard Total International Stock Index Fund to Xtrackers ESG Leaders ETF (EASG), which invests in top ESG companies around the world.

Target Allocation %	Investment	Sub-allocation	Impact Score
38.5% Stocks	Aspiration Redwood Fund (REDWX)	17.50%	5
	Vanguard Total International Stock Index Fund (VTIAX)	12.50%	2
	YieldCos (PEGI, BEP, NYLDA, HASI)	8.50%	5
0% Real Estate	n/a	0.00%	5
2.4% Long-Term Treasury	Vanguard Total Bond Market ETF (BND)	2.40%	2.5
11.6% Intermediate-Term Treasury	Vanguard Total Bond Market ETF (BND)	11.60%	2.5
14% TIPS	Vanguard Inflation-Protected Securities Fund (VIPSX)	14.00%	2.5
14% International Bonds	Vanguard Total International Bond Index Fund ETF Shares (BNDX)	14.00%	2.5
6% Gold	iShares Gold Trust (IAU)	6.00%	2.5
1% Crypto	ETH, BTC, BCH, XRP, ADA, XLM	1.00%	2.5
12.5% Fixed-Return	American Homeowner Preservation (AHP)	12.50%	5

Social Entrepreneur and Sophisticated Investor

The following portfolio is used by a highly sophisticated accredited investor who also runs a social enterprise. The portfolio is highly diversified and balances its higher risk angel investments with income-producing bonds and real-estate investments. The portfolio's impact score is 3.06 out of 5 mainly because of its large proportion in treasury bonds, real estate investment trusts, and commodities, which have nominal impact scores but provide safe growth. The impact score could be improved by shifting some fixed income and real estate to American Homeowner Preservation or Wunder Capital, two fixed return, high-impact investments (however, these funds provide less liquidity based on their 5+ year terms).

Target Allocation %	Investment	Sub-allocation	Impact Score
15% Angel Invesmtents	Multiple private placements	15.00%	5
20% Stocks	Growth Stocks (Amazon, Google)	10.00%	3.5
	Income Stocks (FPI.PR.B, PFF)	7.50%	2
	YieldCos (BEP)	2.50%	5
12.5% Real Estate	Ellington Residential Mortgage REIT (EARN)	2.50%	3
	Blackstone Mortgage Trust, Inc. (BXMT)	2.50%	3
	Welltower Inc. (WELL) Healthcare REIT	2.50%	3
	Weyerhaeuser Company (WY) Diverse REIT	2.50%	3
	Other Real Estate	2.50%	2.5
10.8% Long-Term Treasury	Vanguard Total Bond Market ETF (BND)	0.80%	2.5
	Vanguard Long-Term Treasury Index Fund ETF (VGLT)	5.00%	2.5
	Vanguard Long-Term Bond ETF (BLV)	5.00%	2.5
4.2% Intermediate-Term Treasury	Vanguard Total Bond Market ETF (BND)	4.20%	2.5
2.5% TIPS	TIPS	2.50%	2.5
7.5% Gold	iShares Gold Trust (IAU)	7.50%	2.5
2.5% Commodities	Commodities	2.50%	2.5
7.5% Crypto	Mixed cryptocurrencies	7.50%	2.5
12.5% Fixed-Return	American Homeowner Preservation (AHP 2018)	2.50%	5
	PDQ (Private equity-income)	10.00%	2
5% Store of value	Other Store of Value	5.00%	2.5

Real Estate Investor and Small Business Owner

The following portfolio is used by a small business owner who also invests in affordable housing and adds solar panels. Despite the high-percentage of assets in housing, the portfolio is well-balanced across a handful of sustainable and high-growth potential stocks, income-producing YieldCos like Pattern Energy Group, and a private investment in a solar farm. The portfolio's impact score is 4.78 out of 5. The portfolio's impact could be improved by switching the domestic stock index funds to S&P 500 Fossil Fuel-Free ETF (SPYX), which invests in large U.S. companies while filtering out fossil-fuel producers.

Target Allocation %	Investment	Sub-allocation	Impact Score
7.5% Angel Invesmtents	Private solar farm investment	7.00%	5
	Private placement	0.50%	3
22.20% Stocks	Growth Stocks (SEDG, ETSY, RUN, MGEE, BABA, TSLA, JKS, AY, SPWR, GEVO)	8.20%	4.5
	Diversified domestic stock index funds	3.40%	3
	YieldCos (PEGI)	10.60%	5
63% Real Estate	3 Residential affordable rental properties (with solar panels)	63.00%	5
3.3% Fixed-Return	American Homeowner Preservation (AHP 2015)	1.50%	5
	American Homeowner Preservation (AHP 2018)	1.80%	5
4% Store of value	Cash / High-yield savings	4.00%	2.5

Other Impactful Changes

Here's a list of ideas to help change the world with your money, listed in order from easiest to most involved:

- Switch your bank to the Clean Energy Credit Union, Amalgamated Bank, or Aspiration.
- Move 50% of your emergency savings to CNote, which pays a high-yield interest rate while supporting underrepresented entrepreneurs.
- Review your 401K and know which companies you're invested in. Ask your provider for an ESG fund. Pro tip: Many 401Ks have access to Vanguard funds, which has several great, low-cost ESG funds. (You can also recommend Social K to your employer if they are looking for a more responsible retirement plan provider.)
- If you invest in dividend stocks, shift 50% of them to YieldCos producing renewable energy.
- Invest your next bonus into upcoming entrepreneurs around the world with Working Capital for Community Needs (WCCN).
- Find your local Slow Money and learn about local food companies. Set aside your next $10k for investing in one of them.
- Join an impact investing community like Investor's Circle or Toniic and start learning about impact angel investing.
- Shift your family's foundation investments to 50% community investing through CNote or Enterprise Community partners.
- You're idea here.

Let me know what changes you've made to make a difference with your money, and I'll include them in future updates.

Creating a Better Life, Better World

Let your values guide you. No matter what changes you make, any action you take will move you forward—a better life for you, those who matter most to you, and the world around you.

Designing A World-Class Portfolio— Review

Part 3 gives you the tools to turn your newfound investing knowledge into action.

- Start with your **why**, then your **where** to guide your investing.
- A portfolio's asset allocation is **how** you'll get there.
- The four main investing destinations are:
- Get rich quick
- Long-term, slow-growth
- Short-term, slow-growth
- Preserve your existing money (with income)
- Do-gooder investing is on a spectrum from 0% to 100% and you can choose where you fall.
- All-weather portfolios can supercharge long-term, slow growth investing.
- Short-term investing demands low-risk, liquidity, and returns on pace with inflation.
- You can preserve your existing money and generate income with investments in this book.
- Sustainable and socially impactful investments can often add return while reducing risk in your portfolio.
- Your portfolio is your canvas. Stay in the lines or cover your body in paint and roll around.
- Take an action—big or small—today. I'm challenging 1 million people to shift $10k into more sustainable investments—that's $10 billion together. Sign up at www.adrianreif.com/10k .

The Do-Gooder's $10K Challenge

Up for a challenge? I thought so.

I'm challenging you to take one financial action, big or small, that creates impact and aligns with your values.

Here's the thing: your small action is huge! When one million folks like you take a small action, it adds up.

If 1 million people like you shift $10,000 into sustainable investments, together you'll redirect **$10 billion** towards building a better world.

Report

Once you've made your investment changes, let your fellow do-gooders know. Go to www.adrianreif.com/10k and fill out the anonymous form. We'll keep the number updated so we can show the world that change is coming.

Free Tools

To support you on this journey, you can use the free tools created for you like sample portfolios, links to financial calculators, and spreadsheets with every investment in this book.

www.adrianreif.com/dogoodersguide

The future is yours. Start now.

Outro & F-bombs

I'd considered titling this book "The World-Changing Magic of Giving a F*ck."

...

As a product of the me generation, my parents said "you can be anything you want."

Well, I finally know what I want to be when I grow up.

I want to be a f*ck-giver.

Why?
Because it feels f*cking awesome.

It's fun.
It makes me feel alive.

I can think of nothing more enjoyable than trying to make the world a better place. A bit more clean, just, and joyful.

The world's in the middle of an existential Sudoku.

It needs f*ck-givers. Problem solvers. Joy bringers.

During a conversation once, the other person said, "The world's effed and there's nothing I can do about."

On my lowest days, I succumb to that sentiment. But when I think of this one precious life, I can't think of anything more fun than trying to make the world a little better.

The journey isn't always easy. It's not straightforward. And there is no plan.

It feels like whitewater rafting. Gnarly, invigorating, and exhausting. Sometimes you get tossed out. But we need a shit-ton of us paddling at the same time.

Yes, there are non-f*ck-givers out there. Guess what? Their raft is sinking and you get to carry their lazy asses off. Then, you're going to engineer a way better boat that doesn't sink (while their lazy asses sit there eating chips and squabbling over oil). No. Big. Deal.

It's just what we do.

I've come to understand this is just who we are—and political leadership, shitty news, and naysayers can't change it.

So, thanks for being a f*ck-giver with me. Thanks for seeing the world's existential problems as an adventure.

We have big things to do.

I'm honored to be by your side.

Big love,
Adrian

Definitions

Accredited Investor — The Securities and Exchange Commission has less protection for accredited investors, which is a person who has annual income above $200,000 ($300,000 with spouse) for the last three years OR the person's net worth (with spouse) is over $1 million, excluding the value of their primary home.

Dividend — A dividend is like an interest payment, but technically it's a percentage of a company's earnings. In this book, I've listed dividends as yearly percentages so that we can compare them with interest payments and note payments.

Interest — Interest is the amount of money you earn for lending someone money. In this book, I list interest rates for an annual basis (as they often are). If you lend me $100,000 at 3% interest, I promise to pay you $3,000 per year plus your original principal of $100,000 back.

Non-Accredited Investor — The Securities and Exchange Commission has more protection for non-accredited investors, which is a person who has annual income below $200,000 or whose net worth is under $1 million. Thanks to recent changes through the JOBS Act, non-accredited investors can now access some investment offerings once reserved for only accredited investors.

Note — A note is like a loan with a determined payback. In this book, note will be used to distinguish investments in which you the investor give money to a company or an organization and there is a fixed payback term (length of time) and interest rate.

For example, when you invest in the Calvert Community Investment Note, you are giving Calvert your money for a fixed period of time. If you give it to them for 3 years, they promise to pay you back 1.5% interest on your money each year for 3 years.

A note is different than owning equity (stock) or receiving dividends.

Target Return — Target return is similar to interest, as in the money you can earn on an investment. However, I use "target" when there is not a fixed interest rate and the company or organization is aiming to provide a certain return percentage, but it is not guaranteed. For example, American Homeowner Preservation aims to return you 12% interest per year, but it is based on their performance.

Term — Term is simply the length of time for an investment, usually a note or loan. For example, the Reinvestment Fund has terms of 4 years, 6 years, up to 15 years. Some investments like stock market companies don't have terms, meaning you could buy it today and sell it tomorrow. Other investments have terms so that they have time to do something with the money you've loaned them and they can pay you back with interest.

Acknowledgements

Holy smokes. I thought I was going to sit down and write this book in the solitude of my office while blissfully staring at the mountains, then share it with the world. I had no idea how much of a team effort this would be. My body is purring with heartfelt gratitude, much like I imagine a cat vibrating at the joy of your hands.

Thank you Steve Walker and Ryan Gaines for your indomitable support and prescient feedback. Your precision and intellect amaze me. And your small replies like "I can't wait for this book" were massive motivators. Thanks to Nathan Ottinger for unerringly answering myriad questions, reading many drafts, and receiving my hair-brained ideas. Thanks to those who allowed me to interview them, including Beth Bafford at Calvert, Andrei Cherny at Aspiration, Alex Lamb of New Summit Investments, Katharine Bierce, and Luni Libes of Fledge and investorflow.org.

Thank you to the dozens of folks who answered my early surveys and let me ask them questions. You helped me understand the challenges facing the everyday investors and how we can overcome those. I hope this book justifies your effort.

Dear beta readers, I am sorry for putting you through a half-worked draft and getting my witty attempts at humor out on you. You deserve more than a thanks here for enduring that. But most important, thank you for investing your time in providing feedback. I grew as a writer and a person. Special thanks to Claus Moberg, Asha Aravindakshan, Sere Williams, Dave Drapac, Marie Mainil, Alex Greene, Tom Eggert, Lydia Segal, Steve Burns, Moira Dungan, Bill Sullivan, Jake Jones, Isaac Sinnott, Paul Girgis, Jeff Gowdy, Brian Bengry, and Judy Wagner. If I missed you, deduct three karma points from my ledger and write your name here _____. And thank you.

Mom and Dad, thanks for your unconditional love and support. You always said I could be anything I wanted to be and thankfully I believed you.

Finally, to the most magnanimous mamacita for allowing me to flourish. Laura MF Thomas, life is 3000% better with you. I have no doubt many more people will read *Shit My Zen Teacher Says* and *Finding Magic* than this book.

Endnotes

[i] Younger Generations' Approach to Investing. New York Times.

[ii] Sustainable Reality: Understanding the Performance of Sustainable Investment Strategies. Morgan Stanley Institute for Sustainable Investing

[iii] Does Investing Sustainably Mean Sacrificing Return? Morningstar Research

[iv] The World Economic Forum.

[v] International Energy Agency

[vi] Intergenerational Wealth Transfer, Accenture Consulting.

[vii] "The Good News Despite What You've Heard." Nicholas Kristof, The New York Times.

[viii] Germany Breaks Solar Record. Cleantechnica.com.

[ix] Child Poverty and Adult Success. Urban Institute

[x] Why Diversity Matters. McKinsey & Company.

[xi] Grameen Bank Annual Report 2014.

[xii] The Social Consequences of Homeownership. Robert D. Dietz.

[xiii] Gardening Boom: 1 in 3 Households now growing food. www.farmanddairy.com.

[xiv] Asia Could Run Out of Fish Within 30 Years, UN Biodiversity Report Says. Huffington Post.

[xv] Life Insurance and Market Research Association (LIMRA)

[xvi] Excerpt from *Money: Master the Game*. Tony Robbins.

[xvii] Excerpt from *Money: Master the Game*. Tony Robbins.

[xviii] Money: Master the Game. Tony Robbins.

[xix] Sustainable Reality: Understanding the Performance of Sustainable Investment Strategies. Morgan Stanley Institute for Sustainable Investing

Made in the USA
Middletown, DE
20 September 2020